Voices Rising

PRESS

Cover Art:
by Richard Johnson, ©Richard Johnson 2008
"The Survivor"
Photo collage, colored pencil and acrylic on paper
14 ½" x 14 ¼"
Used by permission

Cover Design:
Bill Lavender

Editorial Assistants:
   For Rebeca Antoine:
      Jennifer Violi
      Zachary George
   For UNO Press:
      Barbara Johnson
      David Parker
      Erin Gendron

Printed in the USA

Library of Congress Control Number: 2007942147

ISBN: 0-9728143-6-1
ISBN 13: 978-0-9728143-6-2

UNO PRESS
University of New Orleans Publishing

Managing Editor
Bill Lavender

UNO Press
UNO Metro College
New Orleans, LA 70148
http://unopress.uno.edu

Voices Rising

Stories from
The Katrina Narrative Project

Edited by
Rebeca Antoine

Contents

Editor's Introduction
Rebeca Antoine   11

We Thought We Made the Right Decision
The Lozanos   17
As Told to Caroline Skinner

Welcome to Oklahoma
Philip Weber   20
As Told to Mary Sparacello

More and More People but No Food
Theron Bolds   25
Interviewed by Zachary George

No Definitive News
Keith Wagner   40
As Told to Nicole Pugh

If We Got on TV Our Families Might See Us
Lux Saturnine   47
Interviewed by Nicole Pugh

In the Same Financial Boat
Michelle Balot   57
In Her Own Words

It Was a Very Peculiar Time
John T. Martin   64
As Told to Nicole Pugh

Even the Crow on the Roof Is Smiling
James Andrew Busenlener   69
As Told to Sylvia Schneller

I'm Not Interested in Talking
New Orleans Police Officer   72
Interviewed by Matthew Peters

The City Wasn't Prepared
Dwight Robinette, Jr.   73
Interviewed by Sheila Willis

Something Terrible Was Happening
Peter Ward 83
As Told to Sylvia Schneller

We Still Didn't Have the Big Picture
Donovan Livaccari 92
As Told to Sylvia Schneller

I Just Need to Get These Old Bones Home
The Ferrara Family 97
As Told by Amy Ferrara-Smith

The House Became an Island
Lora Crayon and Sabrina Avalos 107
As Told by Susanna Dienes

I Was Covering the Story and I Was the Story
Kim Bondy 117
In Her Own Words

We Are Lucky Our House Still Stands
Jana Salmon Mackin 122
In Her Own Words

I Am So-and-So and This Is My Social Security Number
James Welch 127
As Told by Susanna Dienes

Bill You're Alive!
Bill Scheile 133
Interviewed by Nicole Pugh

I Don't Have Friends I Have Associates
Chiquita Carpenter 139
As Told by Dena Vassey

When You're On My Bus You're My Family
Oscar Cade, Sr. 144
As Told to Mary Sparacello

It Was Going to Be a Tiny Little Storm
Rebekah Reuben-Stroup 146
As Told to Amy Judith Reuben Pickholtz

We Have Got to Go
The Belton Family 149
As Told by Dena Vassey

I'm the Leak Expert
Wayne Wilson   158
     Interviewed by Jana Mackin

Didn't You Hear?
Amber Green   167
     Interviewed by Carol McCarthy

This Could Happen Again Next Year
Marjorie and Ralph Guidry   170
     Interviewed by Kristin Schwartz

What Was in That Water?
The Dawson Family   176
     As Told by Amy Ferrara-Smith

What Are We Going to Do With These Old People?
Third Street, Kenner, LA   181
     As Told to Mary Sparacello

Everything Is Scattered
Mary Fleetwood   186
     Interviewed By Eileen Guillory

I Hate the City; I Want to Live in St. Bernard
Sue LeBlanc   193
     As Told by Carol McCarthy

Like Pockets Turned Inside Out
Echo Olander   197
     As Told to Missy Bowen

Us, Two Dogs, a Cat, and a Bird
I. J. Shelton Jr.   204
     In His Own Words

Afterword: Breaches of Faith
Fredrick Barton   216

Interviewers and Writers   246

Editor's Introduction

Rebeca Antoine

On my drive from uptown New Orleans to work at the lakefront campus of The University of New Orleans, I travel down Broad Street. At the corner of Tulane Avenue and Broad Street stands Israel M. Augustine Middle School, a hulking thing built of pale stone with a grand double-sided staircase that leads to a boarded-up door. The sign out front reads: School starts August 18, 2005. That sign always strikes me. Even two years later, as New Orleans chugs along in its recovery from the devastation of Hurricane Katrina, it seems in some ways that time has simply stood still.

Like many others, I thought Katrina would be nothing. I had been recently hired as a lecturer in the English department at Xavier University, and no one at my new job had even mentioned the storm all week, not as they had Hurricane Dennis in the previous month. There was not a word, not even that Friday, August 26, 2005, as I was locking up my office and saying goodbyes to my new colleagues for the weekend. In fact, on that Friday before the storm, I had spent a good portion of what I had left in the bank on groceries for the next week. I wasn't worried because I knew I'd get paid in a few days.

I didn't want to evacuate; I didn't have much money left at the end of August after living off of part-time English instructor pay all summer. When my father called to tell me to watch the weather, I was sure it was nothing. Katrina was going to Florida. On that Saturday before, I woke up late and turned on the news. That's when the fear set in. It was my boyfriend at the time who really wanted to leave. He made a reservation at a motel in Little Rock, Arkansas and convinced me to pool our funds and go. "You don't want to stay here a week without air-conditioning, do you?" he asked.

I left the Sunday morning before the storm hit. The city already felt deserted as I drove down Magazine Street looking, in vain, for somewhere to pick up the money my mother had sent through Western Union to help with evacuation expenses. In the first three hours, I traveled only 16 miles. All told, it took 19 hours to drive the 450 miles to Little Rock, my cat, Othello, sleeping in his carrier on the back seat. There were hours of staring at the same stretch of highway and long trails of taillights, listening to news out of New Orleans on the radio, then more hours on pitch black back roads, and then finally crashing into bed in a city I had never been to before. A day and a half later, CNN made it abundantly clear that New Orleans, my adopted home, was drowning, and I would not be able to return soon. I decided to wait out the uncertainty in my childhood home in Connecticut, where I could relish familiar surroundings and look forward to fall foliage.

But I could not. It is even now hard for me to make sense of the way I felt in those days following the storm. Even though I was far away from New Orleans, anxiety overwhelmed me so much that I had to be prescribed a sedative and was instructed to *stop watching the news*. A week after the storm I was at the wedding of a college friend in Connecticut. It was a trip I had been anticipating for months. I'd bought a new summer suit and was planning to see friends I hadn't seen in years. I've still never worn that suit. Instead, I went to the wedding in an outfit I'd bought the day before because I didn't prepare for anything past the three days I thought I'd be staying in a La Quinta Inn in Little Rock. While standing at that wedding in my brand new dress, I felt uncomfortable in my clothes.

I did not yet know the status of my newly-built New Orleans life. I fretted over my college diploma, though entirely replaceable, and all my fiction writings stored on disks, completely irreplaceable, which, in the rush to leave, I had left on my bed. I did not know if I had lost my new job. I did not know if I would ever be able to come back to New Orleans again. Even though, on a cool September New England evening, I stood at that reception I had been looking forward to, I wanted to go home, and I felt like my insides were crumbling. Fellow wedding guests wanted to debate the government's slow response and the possibility that the levees were intentionally destroyed. At that particular moment, I did not care about arguing the issue.

During that week, I had spent the two days in Little Rock, a few nights at the home of my aunt and uncle outside of Knoxville, Tennessee, and a night at a friend's apartment in Charlottesville, Virginia. And all along the route, on those highways, rain-sodden by the remnants of Katrina, Louisiana license plates were everywhere.

Even though I was able to settle into my parents' home for the duration of my evacuated status, I felt awkward. Family and friends were happy that I was safe, but I wasn't able to be happy just for that, though I tried. I don't know why, for the first month I was away, I pretended I wasn't crying every night, or pretended it wasn't a big deal that I broke down in tears when someone asked me my address. Maybe I pretended because it had not been me on the I-10/610 interchange waiting to be evacuated, because it had not been me rescued from my rooftop. It had not been me at the Superdome or at the Convention Center, and I felt guilty. Maybe I pretended because I was too sad that my city was submerged unforgivably and that all those people with whom I shared a community had been trapped in such deplorable, traumatizing conditions. Those people would never be the same, and the 80 percent of the city that was under water would likely never be the same, either. There was a very real sense that everything would be different from then on, that time would be divided into two eras: Before the Storm and After the Storm.

Ultimately, I did not lose my apartment. I was lucky to live in what Echo Olander calls the "Bubble," what is now popularly called the "sliver by the river," an area that averages about eight feet above sea level and did not flood following the storm. If you never left Uptown, you would never see the damage that Katrina, and the subsequent levee breaches, left behind. I did lose my job and my health insurance. I did lose the boyfriend who traveled all that way with me. In October, I applied for unemployment benefits, which I did not receive until January of the next year, after I'd secured a position at UNO. And I did lose friends to other cities because New Orleans cannot support them with adequately paying jobs and affordable housing. The physical items I did lose to water damage seem paltry in comparison to what so many others lost, many of whose stories are included here.

In this collection of narratives, Mary Fleetwood, an elderly resident of the Gentilly Woods neighborhood, recounts the loss of what has been her home for the last 46 years. Amy Ferrara-Smith relates the poignant story of her family and her 87-year-old grandfather's aching need to see his New Orleans one last time. James Andrew Buselener shows us the event through the eyes of a five year old. In Theron Bolds' narrative, we learn what it was like to be an evacuee in the Louisiana Superdome waiting to be taken somewhere else, anywhere else. Lux Saturnine's harrowing journey through a nearly deserted New Orleans ends on the side of the highway with thousands of others, waiting, hoping maybe to be seen on television so that family might see that she was safe.

The dry but still harrowing French Quarter in those days following the storm is the setting for John T. Martin's and Bill Scheile's stories. Ralph and Marjorie Guidry share the pain of returning to the area after evacuation and their fear that this disaster could indeed happen again. Even though she has returned to New Orleans, Sue LeBlanc has been exiled from St. Bernard Parish, the only place she knows as home. These are just a few of the stories that this life-changing event has produced, and I am grateful to all those who were brave and unguarded enough to share them. My hope is not only that Hurricane Katrina be remembered, but those whom it affected.

This collection comes through the efforts of UNO students who, in the

Katrina semester of Fall 2005, went out and did the important work of collecting and preserving these personal narratives. In many cases, these students worked while they themselves were still evacuated from the city, away from their homes and classrooms. Many of the accounts were gathered in those first few months following Katrina, when the anguish and implausibility of the scope of the disaster was still fresh. My editorial assistants, Jennifer Violi and Zachary George, helped me sort through the hundreds of manuscripts and interviews and were instrumental in narrowing the field to the 31 pieces featured here. We have attempted here to cull a selection representative of the entire collection which is currently housed at the University of New Orleans Library.

My gratitude also goes to the exceptional editorial assistants at the UNO Press, David Parker, Erin Gendron and Barbara Johnson, who have worked closely with Managing Editor Bill Lavender in copy-editing and readying this anthology for publication.

I would like to extend personal thanks to Fredrick Barton for envisioning this project in those days directly following Katrina and for trusting me to see this book to fruition.

Despite all of our losses and grief, our stories are not only about all that is gone. Above the still visible water lines, above the muck and destruction Hurricane Katrina left behind, our voices rise with stories of survival and courage, tales of the generosity of strangers, and the will to rebuild and restore our lives and our city.

November 2007

We Thought We Made the Right Decision

The Lozanos
As Told to Caroline Skinner

The Lozanos rode the storm out until the afternoon of August 30 when they saw the water beginning to rise outside their home. After four days of waiting with little food or water, they were rescued and taken to the University of New Orleans to wait for a helicopter.

Leonard Lozano

I was born on November 6, 1917, and grew up Uptown, around Tulane. I was in the war, enlisted in the Air Corps. I wanted my pick of duty, and it worked out beautifully. I was a clerk in Intelligence. Not everyone can get in the air and bomb people.

We lived in Gentilly for fifty years. Our house was an inheritance from my wife, Audrey. The neighborhood was perfect. The house was perfect. It was just perfect for Audrey and I. We were a half a block from a Catholic Church and a Presbyterian Church. We had restaurants all around us. Our favorite places were Mr. Ed's Deli, Russell's Marina Grill, and the Piccadilly.

I'd been through four hurricanes. I remember Betsy. There were two others. The whopper was Camille. We decided to stay for Katrina because we rode out Betsy with no problem. The morning after the storm was August 30th. We didn't have water over the sidewalk curb. We thought we made the right decision. Unfortunately, a couple of hours later, we noticed water in the street rising; a few hours after that, the rugs in the house were wet. We didn't know how high the water would get. When we had two and a half inches in the house, we got up on tables. There was about six to eight feet in the street. We stayed in the house for four and a half days. We heard on the radio that the levee broke in the Ninth Ward. Then we heard that the 17th Street Canal levee broke.

New Orleans was dead. There was no power at all. No electricity. Nothing. Surprisingly, we slept at night.

At first, I was hopeful and thought everything was going to be OK. But, after a while, it got so still. Rescuers kept passing us up. Then very few were coming by at all. It was quiet. We were really worried. We had very little food. One day, all we had was a glass of cranberry juice, two crackers and half a can of warm Coke. By the fourth day, a neighbor suggested we hang a sheet on our front porch that said, "Please help us." That's what got us rescued at about 5:30 in the afternoon. We got delayed because our neighbors were trying to pack things.

Everything in Gentilly was under ten to twelve feet of water. Everything was wiped out. Ruined. It was impossible to escape the flood. When we crossed Elysian Fields, which is a very, very wide street with a big neutral ground, it was completely covered. Man, it was a lake. Businesses had ten to twelve feet of water in them. Some people were in skiffs trying to ride it out.

They brought us to UNO. There must've been 18 of us just waiting. We kept to ourselves. We comforted each other the best we could. For some reason, they had about five cases of water in the open field. We didn't have anything to eat for two days. Funny though, I wasn't hungry. The stimulant was too great to sleep at all. The best we could do was to doze off.

I didn't fear for my life. You always have faith. But, we lost hope when a helicopter didn't arrive when they said it would. It didn't come till the next morning. Some people were afraid to get into the helicopter. I hope they got rescued some other way.

You know, New Orleans is a very poor city. In my mind, it's gonna take at least two years to come back. It's just being realistic about catastrophes. Audrey and I are lucky. We're able to start over from zero. I can't help but say, my brother, who is 89 years old, was at St. Anna's Nursing Home. They evacuated the patients. Unfortunately, I'm deaf. I worry about my brother. I haven't been able to talk to him. I hope that St. Anna's, which has a history of a hundred and fifty years of service, will get him back. I'm worried he'll die, and I won't find out.

Audrey Lozano

I'm sorry. I thought I could do this, but I can't. I've been trying to forget about that week for three months now, and, listening to Leonard, I don't want to talk about it. You see, it makes it all come back to me. [Her face is flushed, and she is trying not to cry.] Whatever Leonard says, say the same thing for me. Now I have a headache, and it's really bad. I can't remember what I'm supposed to do next. I just don't know. I don't know why in the hell this had to happen to me, but I don't want to talk about it.

Welcome to Oklahoma

Philip Weber
As Told to Mary Sparacello

Philip Weber, with his dog, Spunkie, attempted to ride the storm out on his sailboat in St. Bernard Parish. They were thrown overboard yet managed, improbably, to survive. At the time of this interview, he was undergoing treatment for cancer.

I built my sailboat in Franklin, Louisiana, and I lived on the boat from 1974 until August 29, 2005. The boat was very complete. It had a microwave, a stove, a cold and hot running shower. It had a little fireplace and a piano. Over the years, I have invested a lot of money in the boat.

The Friday before the hurricane, I started getting ready. I put out almost 1,000 feet of lines at the front and back and some shortened lines in the middle. There was a raft of shrimp boats tied nearby, all tied with short lines. They were each twice the size of my boat. They all got loose when the wind went around to the north. It was almost like a tsunami. The water was going up all the time. I went on deck with my dog, which was hard enough to do because the mast had come down. Then one of the shrimp boats hit my boat. The force was so great it knocked me overboard pretty suddenly. The dog found me and jumped on my head, which wasn't helpful. I hung on the side of the boat for a while trying to get back on. I was so tired. I could see at that moment how people died. The water was so high the boat was pushing up against the marina.

I actually swam over my car. My car was ten to twelve feet below me. Waves were up to ten feet. We held on to a cedar tree. I held onto the tree; my dog held on to me. We went up ten to twelve feet every few seconds. All of the shrimp boats were piled up in a shallow marsh. There were probably seventy-five of them within sight. I could see that the nice little restaurant out there now had a boat in it.

On Monday afternoon, a small boat came along with people looking for their shrimp boat. They gave me a ride to the front of the property, to a small hotel. We found a room. The front of the room and the door were gone. Everything was covered with glass and gravel. There were two beds. I pulled back the covers and lay down and slept until Tuesday morning. It was the darkest dark you could ever imagine. There was not a working light bulb within fifty miles of that spot. We stayed there until Friday morning. On Wednesday, I saw some people that were in another building of the motel where they had gone to escape the storm. They had some food. They threw me an apple, and I caught it. I'm the worst catcher, but I caught that. It was so important. Thursday morning, they offered me another apple, which I accepted.

On Thursday, a Coast Guard helicopter landed on Paris Road. They brought with them several MRE's. That was the first real food the dog and I had. I'll never forget it. It was meat loaf with onion gravy. Onions are bad for dogs, so she got the meat and I got the rest. The Coast Guard crew said there would be no more food, so I would have to wade out and evacuate. They thought the water would be low enough to wade out the next morning.

Friday, I put the dog under my arm and started wading. We got all the way up to Chalmette. I thought, "Oh, Chalmette will be dry." It wasn't. The water was about waist deep. There were large trucks with huge wheels that could drive in that water. One of them gave me a ride to the sheriff's station on St. Bernard Highway. It's also the parish prison. There were a number of people in the parking lot. At the Chalmette ferry landing, the National Guard was in charge. I have an edemic leg. My right leg is half as big as my left leg. The Coast Guardsman gave me a piece of rope for the dog. He said that to get on, I had to have a leash for the dog. We went through a chemical fire that had yellowish brown smoke that made everyone nauseous, including the dog.

You could see downtown New Orleans burning. No fire trucks could get there. The ferry landing was pretty much demolished. There was a line of buses. Helicopters were coming in from the Superdome all the time. The bus I got on was called the dog bus because everyone had a dog or a bird or a cat. One lady had three kittens. I got on the bus almost immediately. I thought, "What luck." Not really. We waited hours for them to move us. A National Guardsman jumped on the bus and said, "Everybody down! Somebody is shooting at the line of buses." The guy in charge was yelling at them that "no matter what" they have their duty. "Shoot everyone you see with a gun," he said.

Finally, they moved the buses to another place parallel to the levee and finished their caravan. At that point, every person and all their belongings were searched. I had only the clothes on my back and the dog and one shoe. I lost a shoe while swimming in the hurricane. When we finally got moving, the National Guard was our source of information. They said we were going to the airport in Kenner. For the three days I was in the motel, I had seen C–130's flying east from the airport. They were moving large numbers of people out. I thought, "Wow. Good. Im going to be able to ride on a C–130."

We were met by the Jefferson Parish deputies. They were very sinister. They wore black uniforms, which was fitting because of the way they acted. I can still hear the National Guardsman yelling at the parish police. After a while, the police said we could go. They led the way. The caravan left the airport and went over a railroad yard just to the west of the airport.

Two dump trucks that had been parked to the side of the road pulled in front and in back of the caravan, trapping the buses on the bridge.

Jefferson Parish police had captured a thousand people in 24 buses. I don't know the reason for it. There were about 50–50, people from the Superdome and St. Bernard Parish. They wouldn't let us get off the bus at first. The school buses just don't have any facilities at all. The National

Guard warned us that the Sheriff's Office would shoot anyone who got off the bus. We were refugees not criminals. Even if there was one criminal among us, it wasn't worth treating a thousand people that way. The National Guard told us that a two-star National Guard general would negotiate our release somehow. I assume that happened because around 9:30 or 10:00 Friday night, they decided to release us. The buses just took off. You'd think they were Ferraris, they took off so fast.

They drove us to LaPlace. We traded school buses for luxury-type buses. I went to sleep right away. I learned that we were turned away from Baton Rouge. I woke up in Natchitoches, but we were turned away from there as well; they were full. On my bus, people talked a lot, and I learned that many people had battered through the roofs of their houses when the water came up quickly. In Texas, a group had food set up for evacuees at a roadside park. I got two hot dogs, and so did my dog. I just sat there eating my hot dogs in tears. We got to Dallas and sat there for four or five hours. When we got to Denton, a police cruiser had blocked the entrance ramp.

We ultimately crossed the Oklahoma border. At the first little town we got to, a group of people was waving signs: "Welcome to Oklahoma Hurricane Katrina Survivors." Everyone on the bus was crying. Every time I met a person in Oklahoma, the first thing they said was, "Welcome to Oklahoma." They were the most hospitable people in the most inhospitable circumstances.

On Sunday morning, when it got to be daylight, I found a telephone and called my sister. I just said, "Dianne," and there was about two minutes of silence while we both tried to get a hold of our emotions. I was just blubbering. It was awhile before we could really talk. She had been searching for me on the internet. She is a computer person, and she was really looking for me. They drove me to Cisco, Texas. It was about a six-hour drive. I was released and crossed off the list as rescued.

My sister had an extra house with no renters in it. Right now, I live there alone with my dog. I go to medical appointments two or three times a week. I've had some problems, emotionally, dealing with all of this. I lost everything that I've owned. After 31 years of living on the boat, everything I had was there.

I had a problem for a while with darkness. In the hospital, the nurse would come in and turn off the light, and as soon as she was gone, I would turn it back on. But it is getting better. I got sick from chemicals in the water in Chalmette. At the end of September, I developed blood poisoning. They put me in the hospital, and I don't remember the first two weeks. I was there two months.

I may not make the cancer thing, but I made it through the hurricane.

More and More People, but No Food

Theron Bolds
Interviewed by Zachary George

Theron Bolds is a 35-year-old poet whose writing is tied closely to New Orleans. Reluctantly, he evacuated to the Superdome after deciding that the storm was a serious threat. He describes the chaos and squalor that developed inside the Superdome and his attempts to help others in the face of disaster.

I was at the house watching the news, drinking beer, and then I had dozed off. Woke up about five o'clock on Sunday, and I thought, I can't stay here. I got freaked out. I had thought that there were shelters at the schools. I misunderstood. There were only bus rides from the schools to the Superdome. So I grabbed my big duffle bag and walked some miles to the Superdome. My bag was all heavy, and I was walking and walking with this huge thing. And it starts to rain a little bit. I'm walking and walking, and it starts to rain more and more. Some police drove by and said, "Six o'clock curfew." I'm, like, "All right, six o'clock curfew. I know. I'm just trying to get to the Dome."

I finally get to the Dome around 6:30 Sunday, and it's freezing cold inside. There are people sitting down all over the field, and you have to be processed. Being processed is like going to jail or something. "Put your hands behind your head," they say, and they search you. I had a plastic comb they took.

A plastic comb?

They said, "That's a weapon." I heard that people who had pills on them, if you didn't have a prescription, the police would take them away. I watched this one girl in front of me who had a nail clipper. They said, "Yeah, you can keep it," but they opened it and clipped out the little file inside.

But again, man, [because of the air-conditioning] it was freezing that night.

I was lucky I had a blanket.

And everybody else was all wet, too?

Yeah, there were wet people in there, but there were some people who had got there [before the rain started]. We had to sleep in the stadium on the seats, and they were all talking, and they made this big speech about that we were gonna have food. "We're gonna have food for y'all."

There wasn't that many people. I'd say five or six hundred.

I met this couple, visiting from Canada. They were on their honeymoon, had just gotten married, and they were evacuated from their hotel in the Quarter, and they were told to go to the Superdome. So it was their second night in town. They had just got married. That kind of sucked for them.

But we slept in the stadium that night, you know, slept in the bleachers, freezing. This lady next to me had a radio, and we kept listening to that but weren't really talking much about it.

By this time, we know it's gonna come. It's here; nothing you can do. You better be somewhere safe.

I wake up, like, six in the morning. I stood in the food line forever, but the storm's passing at this point, and I'm sitting in the Dome, and I can hear it, like a train rolling in on top of the Dome. That's just what it sounds like.

Just from the rain and wind?

Yeah, the rain and the wind and windows across the field are exploding.

You could see outside the Dome?

You could kinda see outside the windows, like down where the food was, by the doors. You can't see much, and the lights go off right away. You have the back-up generators with some lights, but now its kinda dark in the Dome, kinda dim, and kinda weird. And I'm sitting in the stadium again, and I'm watching pieces of the roof fly away. It's raining in at this point, so everybody has to move from one section to another, and then that flap goes, so we have to move again, and then another one, so they finally moved us completely out of the stadium.

Who moved you?

The National Guard was around, and they were trying to get it organized. Of course, people were moving anyway because they don't want to get rained on. And it's raining. I'm watching one of these beams swinging, and I'm thinking, Lord, I hope this ain't gonna fly and hit somebody. So I moved, and the storm passed, and it's kind of like the eye is coming on, you know, completely calm.

And this is Monday morning right?

Yeah. Monday morning, day after the storm. And, you know, it's completely calm in the eye. The first part of the storm probably lasted about half an hour. And then I looked out the window, and there's this big satellite dish, like, it's huge. I think it was one of the weather things that track the weather, and it's on the ramp outside the Superdome, and it is blowing off, and I'm thinking, "There goes our weather-tracking device." And there's tree branches everywhere.

And then here comes the other half of the storm, which is worse, so more of the Dome starts to fly away. And everyone is just holding their breath because we can't really see anything and can't go anywhere. It's hot, now. The temperature is rising by the minute [because the air-conditioning is off].

And now the toilets are backing up, and the smell starts to get horrible. There was no more food at this point, and no more water. They couldn't bring any more in through the storm, of course. And everyone is starting to freak out. Then the storm's over, and we were thinking, "All right, we didn't do too bad."

Theron Bolds: Interviewed by Zachary George

And then I thought, "Well, we'll probably be in here for a few days."

Now rumor says this man tried to jump about 50 feet, from a catwalk, but I think he fell because he was sitting on that rail, but that was the beginning of the mess. You know, people started losing it. I mean all over. They wouldn't let us smoke cigarettes, and they wouldn't let us outside. So I go into the bathroom. The men's room is pitch black, but there's a dude with a boombox just hanging out, like it's a club, so we start smoking cigarettes like it's a club. The bathrooms by this point didn't smell too, too horrible, and, sure, everybody wants to smoke, and they wouldn't let us outside. You could hardly breathe. It was really hot.

That night, they finally let us out. There was a big generator out there where people could charge their cell phones. I didn't have a cell phone, though, so I couldn't talk to my family. I didn't know if they made it to where they were going. I don't know if my son and his mom made it to where they were going, so I am starting to freak out, getting madder and angrier by the moment.

It was that night things started to happen, like fights. People were fighting over who was gonna charge their cell phone by the generators. Losing control. The National Guard couldn't handle it. There were old people, sick people, all over the place, lying on the ground.

The food was gone. We could still get a little bit of water, but inside the Dome they started breaking into the refreshments, stealing sodas and stuff. I'm, like, "More power to you," you know. Some of these little dudes were selling sodas to people for two bucks.

And [the National Guard] started announcing, "We have a curfew. You have to be back inside the stadium by one a.m." So I go back in the stadium, and the smell is getting worse, and it's so hot. But there's a little breeze because part of the roof of the Dome is gone, so that was a little refreshing.

And next [Tuesday, the day after the storm] morning, the smell! And it was so hot! You know, it's August in New Orleans. We started hearing stories like "Oh my God, a little girl was raped in the bathroom," or, "I heard a little boy was raped in the bathroom." I'm hearing this, and I'm thinking, I just want to get out of here, now.

While I'm thinking, I notice them bringing more and more people in. And more and more people, and more and more people, and no food, but more and more people. Then they start bringing in some food, but I stood in line for an hour just to get to the front and hear they ran out, so here's two bottles of water. That happened to me a second time, also.

By Tuesday I decided I was not sleeping inside the Dome again. I don't care what they say or what they do. They are bringing too many people in. It's getting really, really crowded. The smell was… I can't even describe it.

It's becoming more and more chaotic because the National Guard is losing control. The NOPD just disappeared. There was one guy I met who was in lockup at NOPD and was just left there.

In lock up?

Yeah. Somebody just opened the door and let them out, and they just walked up to the Dome. Who knows what he was there for? He could have been waiting for a murder trial. Who knows?

Or the 50 other people who were in there with him?

I know, right. He said, "Man, they just left us here to die." I was, like, "That's just horrible."

I was starting to learn different things around the Dome, like where I could go to find water, where the stockpile was. By this point, you had to walk through the Dome covering your nose because of the smell. The floor was covered with blood and urine and feces and everything else, little kids walking around with no shoes, glass everywhere. I mean definitely every kind of disease was just livin', breathin' right there.

So yeah, I slept outside on the ground that night, right outside the Dome on the ramps.

Was anybody with you?

Yeah. I met this one cat and his mom, but he was kind of weird because he was, like, looking at girls, like we was hangin' out in the club. I was, like, "Dude, this is not the time." So I had to get away from him, and I was by myself for the most part.

I was outside on the ground, and I was camped out a few feet from where a troop of guardsmen were camped, while a whole bunch of other guardsmen were walking around. That was when I heard about the guy being shot in the legs inside the Dome, and I was thinking, we been hearing so many rumors, who knows?

So the Guard is lining up, doing their drills, and before I know it they scream, "Make a hole!" And they start running, and whoever's in the way just gets knocked down. One guy fell on me. I hit my head on the wall. Another guy hit his head and started bleeding. It was chaos, dude. And this was Tuesday!

So after that I decided, not only am I not going to sleep inside, I'm not going to sleep, period. You know what I'm saying? I found a friend of mine, and he sat with me, and I must've dozed off about four or five in the morning, and I woke up around six.

I gave up on the food thing, like, "I don't care, just give me water." I was keeping little bottles of water and making them last the whole day. My blanket was lost by this point. So I decide, "All right, I gave up my blanket."

I met this guy and his wife. I see his wife lying on the ground, like, trembling and shaking. She's on some sort of medication. They had their dogs with them. People were bringing their dogs. And I see helicopters bringing more people in, and I start hearing about the levee breaking. And

I'm like, "Well you know, I'm looking down the street, like on Poydras, and I don't see water. Just let me out. I'm ready to go."

So Wednesday morning, I see these kids soaking wet. I gave them [some of my extra] clothes. Then I gave their grandparents my [remaining] clothes, so I end up hanging out with them. We kind of make camp together. It was a horrible situation, but we became a crew and started working together, and that was kind of cool.

But I'm still thinking I want to go. So the National Guard guys are like, "You can leave if you want to, but nobody's gonna come get you if something happens, so you won't be rescued."

Then this one guy standing next to me decides to leave. 15 minutes later he came back, soaked up to his neck.

And it wasn't raining?

Oh no. It was bright sunny outside. It was hot. He said he stepped down off Claiborne [Avenue] into a river. He said he didn't know the water was that deep. And I'm, like, "Dude, that's just nuts." So I can't leave. I don't know what's gonna happen. Nobody does.

Were there any televisions?

No. There was no power really. [We had] a radio, and we were all waiting for the governor to make a speech. But when she finally gets on the radio, she has nothing to say. We'd all been waiting for her.

So it's getting hotter; people are getting more frustrated, more rumors, more people crying, and you see people who just lost their families, who've been rescued from their roofs. And by this time, I'm a veteran; I know where stuff is.

It's Wednesday?

Yeah. I'm going over to where they bring people in just to get air from the helicopters because it was so hot. I see people with these blank looks on their faces, man. I'd just give them big hugs. They were, like, they lost their whole families. One guy said, in order to rescue his kids, he had to throw them from the roof into the water and hope he could rescue them that way. I don't know if they all made it. They were little kids, you know. That made me think I didn't have it so bad.

I see sick people laying on the ground in all that nastiness. So whatever food I got I would give to them, but I needed water. And then I thought, you know, I have to eat something in order to maintain.

Then some people started to leave. There was a big crowd of people waiting to get on a bus, but I didn't get into the crowd because things were happening there. People fighting, pushing, passing out from the heat. And these people stood there for hours and hours.

Helping people, that was my way of keeping my sanity, you know.

I'm camped out on the second level on the ramp, right across from New Orleans Center, where the radio broadcast was. By this time it's thousands of people from every walk of life. You've got murderers, drug addicts with no drugs, crackheads with no crack; you know that's bad.

[I met] a friend I knew from years ago; I started talking to him. He was, like, "Dude, I'm a heroin addict. Do you know where I can find some?" Normally I would just walk away, but I was, like, "Dude, I do wish I could help you."

He needed it.

And again, there are people, you know, people who need medications, like diabetics.

The National Guard is overwhelmed. There's nothing they can do at this point. The ones doing the search and rescue missions, they're being attacked by people in the neighborhoods. They're being shot at while they're trying to rescue people, so they had to give that up

Why do you think that was? Because they were rescuing some people and not others?

Because it was a whole chaotic situation. From the people in the street I'm finding out what's going on out there. And I could tell them what's going on in the Dome, and when we talk, I can tell there's not much difference. It's craziness. We could hear explosions in the background. And you got gun shots, you got fires everywhere, you got smoke, you got helicopters. People screaming and crying and all kinds of things, and meanwhile I just kind of sit there and wait.

And while all the focus is going to that craziness outside, inside the Dome, we're suffering. We got no food, no water, but they're trying to stop looters, which to me was… It pissed me off, honestly.

People were bringing in [looted] clothes and hanging them up to dry, and I didn't think that was too bad. People needed shoes and clothes. People were walking around with those MRE bags for shoes, you know. And you could hardly walk anywhere because of the trash, and if you're not stepping over trash, you're stepping over people.

By this time, I could see the water on the street. It's Wednesday evening, and the night times were the worst. Wednesday was probably one of the worst. Police were everywhere. Every time you made a camp, police were waving guns, yelling, "Everybody move." Guns in your face every day.

Were people talking back to the police?

Well, people were being chased. People were running from the police into the Dome without being processed, and they just kind of overwhelmed the post where the National Guard were. They were just, like, letting the people come in, but some of these people were coming in with guns and shit. So, you know, it's scary, and fights breaking out. And then you hear things like people saying, "My God, I just found out that so and so is dead, but at least we know." Just relieved to know.

And I still didn't know anything about my family. I almost broke down, but, you know, you have to keep it together. And, right at that moment, I'm looking down at the water, and this guy says, "I hope that's not what I think it is." And I was, like, "I hope not either." And I look down, and I swear, dude, there was a body, and it was just floatin'. It was right outside of the Superdome. It was just horrible

I have to go inside the Dome still to get food and water. It was like something out of a horror movie. There was a literal fog inside. It was misty. You could see blood on the floor. You could see urine and shit. It was really dark, and there was that fog, and there were people lying on this floor, just passed out. Some were dead; some were just unconscious. There were no medics to help people. There was a woman on the floor of the bathroom some little kids told us about, and we picked her up and brought her out. Some people had brand new babies, inside on this floor, and all you could do is walk around and step over them.

You wanted to help everybody, but if you try to help everybody it's just way too overwhelming. So I am looking at it like little bits of time. What can you do? Just try to stay with the people you're with and try to help each other and hope that everyone else is doing the same thing.

Of course not everybody was. Let's say, for example, there is a lady lying on the ground. If she's got a purse, they're gonna take her purse. Somebody's gonna rob her. So my attitude was not only looking for food and water but....

Like, you wanna help people, but at the same time you kinda don't want to touch people because you don't wanna touch... whatever, you know. You want to keep your face and mouth covered as much as possible, and whatever you need to get you get as quickly as possible.

There's more and more food and water now because more people are getting out, but more shit starts happening, more and more fights break out, more and more crowds of people. I watched this one old guy sitting above the parking garage, drinking. He had to be drunk because he looked like he finished a whole fifth of Jack or something, and I watched him take the last swig, and he fell down and his head busted open. He wasn't dead, but he hit the ground, SMACK, and you heard it. And I was like, "I knew it." And then the blood, and they had to come rescue him. This was like Wednesday and Thursday all of this was going on.

By Thursday, I guess, to control the looting, George Bush ordered the military to, like, bomb the city. Well, not really with bombs, but here was this dude who was from the military, and he used empty grenades to kinda, to distract them or whatever. But you heard big booms, and it's like a war. You heard helicopters and saw fires and smoke and people screaming and crying and shooting and guns in your face every five or ten minutes. This guy I was camped out with, he was in Vietnam, and he was like, "The only difference is I don't have my own gun."

There was one dude who came running through the Dome talking about, "All right I'm gonna get y'all out of here." And we saw him go in, and we never saw him again.

We heard the mayor make his big speech. He's talking, he's cursing, he's all upset, and everything else. It was definitely inspirational. It was good to finally hear somebody speaking up for us. He saw the situation, and he was horrified just like anybody else would be.

But after this we are listening to the radio, and all we hear is, "All right, this one needs to do it. No it's the federal government. No, it's the state." And I don't care who does it. Don't play politics while people are literally dying inside the Dome. I mean I never seen nothing like people dying from no injuries, just being sick. People on medications, or addicts. If they're not dying, they're freaking out, trying to kill somebody else because there were drug dealers selling bad drugs or fake drugs or whatever, making people sick. There's drug wars, different neighborhoods having conflicts with each other. And the politicians were so calm on the radio, like, "Oh, you know, New Orleans people were evacuated. What do you think will happen if another storm comes?"

I'm, like, "Dude, this storm was four days ago!" We're not talking about next year. Who cares? Get us out of the Superdome!

This was Thursday, my fifth day in the Dome, and Thursday night somebody got shot and killed. Nobody believed it, but the National Guard guy told me it was true. You'd be in the middle of a conversation and hear POP POP. For five minutes you feel like everything is cool, and then you gotta run. By my fifth day I knew when to walk and when to duck.

I was standing around and saw this white guy wearing glasses, and he takes this kid by the hand and just starts to walk away. And I was, like, "What's that all about?" So they went and caught that guy and started beating him because he was trying to take this kid to do whatever.

It wasn't his kid?

Oh no! This was a white dude. And a little black kid about 6 years old.

Oh shit.

And this white guy just walked by and kinda walked off, but we noticed it, and these guys grabbed him, and they were about to throw him over the ramp and into the street but the National Guard guys caught him and saved his ass. But shit like that was happening a lot. Child molesters.

Finally Friday the Air Force came in, and these dudes were older cats because the National Guard, they were like kids who just wanted to pay for college, and here they are stuck in the Dome just as horrified as we were. They got guns but they're in tears. It got to the point where I was going up to the Guard guys like, "Dude, you need anything? You okay?"

You see the faces of the people brought in by helicopters, just blank faces. My God, everybody looks like ghosts. Everybody looks like zombies walking around. Some people, all you could do is walk them around and have them sit somewhere.

But when the Air Force finally came, they got the crowd that was in front of the Dome together to get on the buses. They kind of got things in order. You know, it's the Air Force. It's the older guys. They're, like, no nonsense kind of guys. But still, I was, like, "I'm waiting. I've been here all this time, and I really don't want to go to Houston, so I'm gonna just sit on it."

I remember that Friday, this guy I know had been inside the Dome with his mom and his sister and his grandma, and he had been there as long as me. And he was like, "Dude, my grandma is sick. She needs help. She's 80 years old. We gotta get her to a medic." So I helped him carry her on an army cot over to the MASH helicopter Red Cross thing, and they were, like, "No, we don't have any medics, but we'll take her."

So there were no medics. This is four days after the storm, and there's nothing. There's no help. The only thing is to get us out.

The attitude inside was, like, "I hope I don't die today." Could today be the day? Am I gonna get shot? Is this whole thing going to explode? Is it gonna turn into the military versus the people? Because it was becoming… It was getting that way. The military was losing patience and feeling threatened. I really thought it was going to turn into us against them.

Yeah, man, I finally got out Friday night about 10:30. We finally left. And by that time I had to get rid of my shoes because….

Funky?

I was so horrible, bro'. I had on the same socks and clothes for the same six days.

So I get on this bus, and I don't know where I'm going, and I am just drained. And as soon as we get there to the Westbank [just across the Mississippi River, about five miles from the Dome], there's lights, there's power, and we're, like, "What's this all about? Why couldn't we be somewhere like this?" They have stores and stuff. It looked like nothing had happened.

And it had been like that the whole time?

Yeah, the whole time. And I'm just, like, "What the hell is going on, and where are we going?" I'm barefoot at this point, and it's late at night, so finally I sleep.

So we're driving, driving and, a wonderful thing, we stop in Texas to get gas, and there's a diner next door, tiny, and this guy goes in and [comes back out saying], "Hey, somebody's gonna buy us food!" And I'm, like, "Another rumor," you know. Then the bus driver says, "Yeah, somebody's gonna buy us breakfast!"

So the people in this diner are not staffed for 100 people smelling like god-knows-what, filthy, and hungry, but they cranked it out. They were just so helpful and so generous, just a beautiful, beautiful thing.

I went in the diner and I was, like, "Who did this?" And it was one guy. And I guess they called people because truckloads starting coming in, church groups, and they started showing up at the restaurant with toothbrushes and diapers and socks and shoes and clothes. Just amazing people.

Shows you how beautiful people are, even though…

The government sucks. Yeah, man, I was never so happy in my life for a toothbrush and toothpaste.

I didn't wake up until we got to Oklahoma. It was, like, 1:30 in the morning, but they were ready. They had hot food. There's about 600 people on this military base, but there were showers, and finally we got to sleep with, like, real clean sheets.

They have TV's in the mess hall, so I was able to watch the news, and, for the first time since before the storm, get some information. First time seeing pictures of the Superdome from the outside.

There were computer labs set up, and an infirmary, and the Red Cross was amazing. And us, the people from the Dome, we were so in this frame of mind to help people that we needed to be doing something constantly, you know, and that just wouldn't go away. It was constant. So I stayed there in Oklahoma for five days.

Finally I talked to my family and decided to go to Santa Fe. It was cool on the military base. They were, like, if you want to stay, there's schools, and we can get you jobs. But my mom bought me a bus ticket to Santa Fe.

It was real sudden. I didn't even say good-bye to the people I was camped with. Everybody was eating lunch, and I just left. I got on the bus, and I was feeling great. I was, like, "Finally."

No Definitive News

Keith Wagner
As Told to Nicole Pugh

Keith Wagner is a technical writer who lives in the French Quarter and stayed in his home for nine days after the storm hit. Wagner and his neighbors shared resources and worked cooperatively but were concerned for their safety. Violence and lawlessness grew rampant as people became more desperate and law enforcement more overwhelmed.

I really didn't pay that much attention to it. It was just another hurricane. It was on the morning news, but I really didn't look at it at all that weekend. My sister called Sunday morning and said that they were evacuating to Covington to go to our parents' house. She said I had ten minutes to make up my mind; either she was going to come get me, or I would stay. I didn't have a car or anything. If I was going with them, she was coming right there and then. I said, "No. I'm staying. It will pass in a day or two. It will turn around." Last year, during Ivan, we all ran away and did the whole hide-out thing for three days. When we got back, it took us longer to unpack than it did to go out. I did laundry and got groceries, the usual kind of stuff. I really didn't watch the news and didn't know that much about where it was coming from or how big it was.

Of course, as it was coming through—I think it was early Monday morning—I was watching the morning news. Then the air conditioner stopped, and all the power was off. I was like, "Oh no! It really happened." But I still felt like, "Oh well, five minutes and the power will come back on."

[That night] was very noisy and very scary. At some point, water was coming through my bedroom ceiling and down the living room wall. What had happened, I found out later, was the windows upstairs had flung open and water was just coming through the open windows. It was dripping onto the fan and onto my bed. I remember pulling all the laundry I had done, which was on the bed, and all the bed covers, onto the floor because it was wet.

Somewhere in the middle of the day, Darryn, a neighbor, came over, and we moved some of my living-room furniture out of the way of where the water was dripping down. Then we went to his house. His roof had caved in. The wind was intense, and shingles were flying off. The rain was coming in sporadic bursts. At one point, we were running down the street, looking for someone with their door open. One guy opened his shutters. The shutters blew off the hinges and flew down the street. He pulled us in and gave us dry clothes to change in to. We were sitting there, and a huge tree came down in his back yard, right against the back French doors. That was the hurricane.

After a while, the wind died down. We were like, "That wasn't so bad." We went out and had a couple of drinks. The power was still out. It got hotter and hotter. On Tuesday, many of the neighbors got together and took off to Jackson [Mississippi]. Suddenly, several of my friends were gone.

No one knew that there was flooding all around us. All I had was a little tiny battery radio that would stay on for a while and then fade out. At some point, WWL had relocated to Baton Rouge. After that, it was just a call-in. Mostly people were just calling in and complaining. It was doing more to ruin my spirits than it was to help. Most of the time, I turned it off because there wasn't anything to help me really, no definitive news.

There was nothing to do but go outside and talk to each other. Everybody would come out to the sidewalk, and we sort of checked out how many people were still on our block and the next block down towards Matassa's [Grocery]. We walked around a little but not much. There weren't any police around or anything. Once it became dark, it was very dark. It was becoming more and more violent.

On Tuesday, several people came by to say that the Winn Dixie was giving away all their water and food supplies. Of course it turned out that that wasn't the case. Still, four or five of us walked down there. We kind of just followed this horde of sheep walking there. Once we hit Rampart, the water from there to the parking lot of the Winn Dixie was a foot deep. We walked in and realized that all of the front doors had been pulled off. People were in there stealing and no one was actually handing out anything. They were throwing bottles of pickles on the floor just to watch them explode, opening bottles of brandy, wine, and whiskey and drinking them right there, then throwing the bottle on the floor after they were finished. There was glass all over. I took one look and turned around and left. I walked home by myself. I was afraid of being arrested. I was afraid of getting killed or beat up, or who knows what else. I came back home as quick as I could.

The police station on Rampart isn't too far from there, and there wasn't a police car to be seen. Obviously, it was chaos and nobody was doing anything. I lost all respect [for the police]. I later found out that a few people had been killed on their way home, bringing canned goods back. A lot of people were stealing things for the heck of it, taking things out and throwing them in the parking lot.

On Wednesday, I decided I would clean out the refrigerator because it was getting warm and smelly. I took everything out, lugged it out and threw it away. Then we cleaned out two of the places across the street because we had the keys to all these different places. Directly across from my house, on the opposite side by the school, we made a trash pile. That was where we took everything from the fridges and our trash cans. We just made a 20 foot long trash pile. It grew and grew and became the designated spot for all of it. Of course, we still went walking and talked to people on the next block to find out how many people were still around. People who had a lot of water shared it with other people. We had a couple of places where people filled up bathtubs before the hurricane. As the days wore on, we wore the same T-shirts, the same shorts. We didn't take baths. There was no place to shave, no place to wash, no bathrooms. That became a real big problem.

Concerning that issue, you get really creative. You use the back yard, the courtyard, you put fresh bags in a trashcan and that becomes a toilet. Some people used the water from the tubs [to flush]. *only this done*

Towards the end of the week, they started the curfew. I am not sure what night it was, Thursday or Friday. We tried to talk to the cops, but they just said, "Get out of here! Get out of here!"

On Thursday, my neighbor next door and I walked as far as Canal Place. They had said if we could get to Harrah's, they would have water and food and buses. The police turned us away. They were camped out at Harrah's. Under an awning, there were palates and palates of bottled water and palates of bags of ice sitting out in 105-degree heat. The piles of ice were four or five feet high. They wouldn't give us anything.

The ice and water were for the police. That was the morning that Saks was on fire and had been looted. Brooks Brothers was looted and burning. Of course, the fire trucks were lined up, but there wasn't any water. They weren't doing much good. Whole racks of clothes from Brookes Brothers were just dragged out across Canal and thrown into the street.

A different neighbor and I walked back on Friday morning. This time, we did get as far as the Convention Center. That's when the National Guard finally came out for the very first time. On the right side of the street, as we walked past Harrah's, there was block after block of black people—young, old, ladies, kids—standing out with chairs and blankets and things. We were walking in the big parking lot on the other side of the Hilton. They were waiting for buses. They were waiting for something. We went on the other side of the parking lot, and the National Guard was unloading palates of food and water. There were probably a couple thousand bottles of water, MRE's and things. They were bringing in the trucks with the porta-potties and all the food.

The National Guard was really nice. They gave us two bottles of water each *Friday* and MRE's. They told us that we could stand in line further down, and they were going to have helicopters come in and take us out. But you couldn't bring any pets, and you couldn't take anything with you. It was just you and no belongings. Since my neighbor was walking his new puppy with us when we went up there, of course we weren't going to get on the buses or helicopters.

We were starting to give up hope that anybody was ever going to come. My phone didn't work; we couldn't get a signal. Most people's cell phones had run out of charge. My mom was able to call me. She started to call me at ten in the morning and six at night. My sister in Nashville relayed with her, and then she emailed my sister in Tucson.

There were long hours with nothing to do. Every time you walked around, you would see the police just sitting there, doing nothing, pointing guns at you. If you went up to them to ask them a question, you suddenly had a rifle in your face. Until the National Guard came around. They were the ones who would drive around every day. They would stop and talk to us. They mostly said that they had no idea what was going on, and they didn't know where to get help. We couldn't get anyone to take us out. The guys next door had a puppy, and no one would let them take it so they couldn't get out. Finally, a reporter from the AP was doing a story, and he agreed to take them out and drop them off wherever. So they took off with him.

Slowly, on every block, people either walked out of town, got on the bus, or someone with a car somehow was getting them out.

We got to the point where we were running out of food. We still had water, and people were going over to Johnny White's Bar and drinking hot beer or whatever was around in people's kitchens. As they left, we would get their keys. I think I had keys to seven houses by the time I finally got out of here. It was good because you couldn't do any dishes. If we did make some soup or heat something up, we would have a house where we could cook something. Then we would go to the next house and get clean dishes.

We just left the dirty dishes behind. My kitchen, of course, was a disaster. The dishes sat in the sink and on the counter for six weeks.

Hard as it is to believe, folks in the Quarter during that time found ways to have a little fun and let loose. Labor Day was a good excuse for a party and a parade.

They were going to do the parade for the festival that would have been that weekend. I think six to eight people made a little tiny parade and pitched around for two or three blocks. People waved them on from their houses.

We saw kids running down the street stealing trashcans and things from the yards. All the gates and things blew off of people's houses. Periodically, these kids would leave wagons. Some guy left something from Friedman Decorating Company. Someone said, "Oh, it's a float. We will decorate it." And it became a float. We would salvage things. They had a couple of people dressed up and they rode to Johnny White's and then back down. That night, someone found three or four bottles of red wine in someone's house. We sat on the sidewalk, about seven or eight of us. We just sat out until curfew and talked.

Helicopters started finally flying over Saturday and Sunday night [a week after the storm]. They would illuminate the entire street and light up the entire block. The cops would drive by, looking for people. If you were outside, [after curfew] they yelled at you, shot you, or hauled you away. We got yelled at one night. It was one minute to eight. We were going to stay on the balcony because we had been sleeping on the second floor with the balcony windows open. This way we could get just a little bit more air. They came around with the helicopter and shined the lights right on top of us.

On Monday afternoon, we were walking around. By this time, we would venture out and walk three or four times a day—to the river, to the French Market, down to Canal Street. That afternoon, I was walking and I saw the Red Berets marching. It was the most wonderful sight in the world.

They were all in their military riot gear with their red berets on. There were hundreds of them and they were on both sides of the street, marching block after block. It was the greatest sight in the world. They stopped and talked to me, asked me where I lived, and asked me if I ever heard gunfire. I started walking with them. They all turned and came up Orleans Street, and then they came up here [to Dauphine Street]. We walked up and down Dauphine, and I showed them the areas where we had heard gunfire.

I told them about the night I sat on a balcony across the street and watched a guy sit down on my front steps, eat a bag of chips, load his gun and walk off. Two days before that, I heard gunfire out front, mostly on the corner of St. Ann over towards Rampart. That whole area was really big for gunfire. The Red Berets said, "Don't worry, you can sleep tonight. We will be sitting here on your doorstep. If you hear gunshots, it will be because we shot someone. It won't be anyone firing a gun at you." I slept in the entryway of the house here. I pulled all my bedroom stuff out in the entryway. By then, it was all wet and molded. I pulled the comforter out, and I kind of padded it with a couple of pillows. It was probably about 110 degrees. They were out there all night long.

On Tuesday morning, we figured out how to boil coffee on the gas stove. This was our last day, and we actually made coffee without electricity. We talked, and then we went out and walked around. My neighbor had gotten his car back somehow. Everybody was saying that the roads were still closed, and nobody could get in or out. Then at about 10:30, we found out that one of the bridges going out was open. So then it was, "You have five minutes. Grab your toothbrush." Of course, I grabbed the cats across the street. My friend knew we had to take them. And he took a lot of his birds. We put the cats in the carrier. I took my T-shirts and a pair of shorts and something for my contacts and my glasses, locked the door, drove off and hoped that I would come back.

If We Got on TV Our Families Might See Us

Lux Saturnine
Interviewed by Nicole Pugh

Lux Saturnine is a bartender at Flanagan's in the French Quarter and lived in an uptown apartment when Katrina hit. She and a few friends remained in the city during the storm and then endured a frightening and bizarre exodus from New Orleans.

I had no idea there was even a storm coming. I have one TV, and it is attached to my VCR. I play Playstation on it, and then I put it away. I don't watch it. I don't listen to the radio [...] And I do all of my socializing in bars.

Where the information is questionable.

Very questionable.

So when did you finally realize that the hurricane was coming?

Saturday. I was like, whatever. I have lived here for five years, and there have been, what, 11 hurricanes since then? Nothing ever happens. During Ivan, I sat in a lawn chair on my balcony on Magazine Street with a case of Rolling Rock, getting drunk, waiting for something to happen. I think it rained for 20 minutes. It was ridiculous. Tornados are scary. Hurricanes, big deal.

I got home from work on Saturday night, and my roommates were gone. My landlord was gone. Usually, he will board up the house. Even for a tropical storm, he boards up the windows for us. Nothing was done. I turned on the news, and it was a category five, the end of the world; we are all going to die; deep shit; entire city wiped out; five years to recover. Okay, I thought, maybe a tenth of this is true. I am going to board up the house. I didn't have any plywood, so I took all the doors off everything, all the closets, all the inside doors of the house. I put them up against the windows.

Were you by yourself?

I was with my boyfriend. We were going to stay at my house. We picked my house because it has been there forever, and we figured it was going to be there forever. Later on, that turned out to be a bad plan. I live on the third floor. It's an attic that has been converted into an apartment. The house started shaking…it sounded like a freight train was coming through it. We ran downstairs and kicked open the second-floor neighbor's apartment door. She has this hallway that has doors on either side. We figured that it had to be structurally sound. It was only three in the morning at that point. The hurricane was not even supposed to be there until eight in the morning, yet it sounded like we were going to die. We couldn't call someone. We couldn't even turn on the news to see if it was here yet. We were thinking it couldn't possibly get any worse, so it had to be here. Every hour, it got worse. We could hear windows being torn out and all kinds of insane racket, things flying through the air outside the house. Balconies were flying off, and crap from the neighbor's yard was flying in. Doors were slamming so hard they were coming off their hinges. My entire house wound up cracking in half. It shifted up three inches. We were scared shitless to come out of there. The one window that didn't break was to an adjoining bathroom. It was this huge picture window, totally exposed. And we had to go into the bathroom periodically. We would run into the bathroom, jump into the tub, and then jump out, trying not to get killed the whole time. All we saw was a hallway and a tub for 12 hours.

Of course, later on, when we got to my boyfriend's shitty modern apartment above a bar, it was fine. There wasn't even a window missing. We could have stayed there the whole time.

We came out of the hallway around three in the afternoon. The wind was still flying around. My house was wrecked. Everything was destroyed. When my window broke, it toppled my bed over, and my mattress fell on top of a big pile of clothes. That turned out OK. I was able to salvage most of my clothes.

On Tuesday, we slept for like 20 hours. We were wiped out from being stressed out for that long. There was a guy who lived behind us, and he was still in town. He stole a grill from the neighbor's yard, and we grilled whatever was in our fridge that was going to go bad.

There were a few people around you that had stayed?

There were three others: the next door neighbor, the neighbor behind me, and the downstairs neighbors. It was totally dark. Usually, there is this orange glow when you look up [at night]. That was totally gone. We could pick out constellations looking at the sky. We saw falling stars. It was absolutely gorgeous. We had no idea that anything bad was going on. I mean, the power was out, but the power goes out here if the wind blows. You learn to deal with that. We figured that the power would be out for about a week, not that bad. It was out for about a week after that crappy tropical storm [Cindy] came through.

Then the water went out. Apparently, they turned the water off because there were dead people in it, but we didn't know that yet. We decided to leave my apartment. We walked up to my boyfriend's house, about twenty blocks, carrying all of our stuff.

Did you have any idea that the water was rising?

No. We didn't know that there was water at that point. I think it was about three o' clock that day [Wednesday] when we went to the bar across the street, Ms. Mae's. They were open. There were dozens of people there. They were storing their beer in the ice machine. As long as they had ice, they were going to stay open. We started having community meetings there. We decided that every day at three, everybody who stayed in the Garden District would meet up there. We had one radio, and somebody had a battery-powered television. That's how we found out that the levee had broken. When people found out, shit totally hit the fan. Everybody went insane. They lost their minds.

One guy who was in this bar, Don, had ridden his bicycle to the Garden District [from the French Quarter]. We ran into him on Wednesday afternoon, and he said that all of our friends and co-workers were down there with guns. We thought, that's settled; we are going to go there. The next morning, we got up at like seven and got together a backpack, a bottle of water, the necessary things for a day trip. We started walking down to the Quarter. We made it about four blocks, and there's a dead body. We made it about three more blocks, and there's a dead body. We went about five more blocks, and there's a dead body. This time, it is someone I know. That was the end of that. We turned right around and went back into our house. We locked ourselves inside. We were not going to go anywhere.

They were dead because of the flooding?

No. People were shooting each other. We came across a guy who had been stabbed recently, like that day. Some of his friends said that this guy had been walking around with a serious injury for hours. He was bleeding to death. No one could find any help for him. He just died in the road. Some people in the neighborhood buried my friend.

We heard that there was an evacuation point near our house, like five blocks away. We were debating whether to go there or not. We were afraid that if we went there, they would take us straight to the Superdome.

So you had heard about that?

Word got around really fast about the Superdome. You know, just by people talking to each other.

So then what?

There was this old man that would show up every day at the community meetings. His name was Mr. Neighbor. He probably couldn't walk more than two blocks on his own. He wanted to leave. He was ready to go. He had been sitting there every day, day after day, with his little bag that had all his disability, social security and veterans' benefits information in it. That was all he needed. He was just waiting for someone to get him out of there. It was so sad. We began to devise all these plans to get him to the evacuation point. We went there and tried to talk the people into driving to where he was to get him because it was only like five or six blocks. We couldn't get anyone to do it. We thought about getting a shopping cart and pushing him there. But he didn't want to do that. It was horrible. We spent two days trying to figure out how to evacuate this poor old guy. Finally we went to the evacuation point and they are like, "Look, if you get on this bus, we'll take you to Lafayette. No cattle shoot, no insane refugee camps. We will take you straight to Lafayette, and we will put you in a hotel."

So we got on the bus. But we are still like, "Please go get this guy." They wouldn't go three blocks out of their way so they could get him. We saw him as we were driving by. It was heartbreaking, until we got where we were going and realized that we were glad he didn't come with us. Instead of driving us to Lafayette, they took us to Kenner and kicked us out on the side of the road with about 4,000 pissed off, hungry people, no shade, no water, no information about what was happening to them. There was nothing.

Where was this?

It was at I-10 and Causeway. Their brilliant idea was to put a bunch of people in a shit-filled swamp and see how long it will take for them to get pissed off and riot like they did at the Superdome and the Convention Center.

Who were the people who were organizing the evacuation?

We saw police and military. They dumped us in the middle of nowhere. It was never about evacuation. It was about putting everybody in one spot so they can keep an eye on him or her. I'm there with my boyfriend and 4,000 pissed off, lower-class, poor black people. The first thing I heard was some guy passing by, saying, "Motherfucking white people won't let me leave." I thought, I am going to die. They are going to kill me. They are pissed off, and it's my fault because I am the only white person here. I was really fucking scared at that point. Then we saw some people we knew. We ran over. It was seven or eight of my friends who worked in other bars. One of them had just come from the Superdome. He escaped at gunpoint, the military saying that they were going to shoot him if he left. He said, "Fuck you," and dodged through hallways. He swam six blocks to get to the Garden District and got picked up by one of these evacuation buses. He had already been to the Superdome, so when he got to Kenner, he just totally lost his mind. He started drinking and drinking and drinking. We couldn't make him stop. We eventually had to leave him. We were like, "Look, we have to stay alive here. We can't babysit you. Fend for yourself." That was the second time I had to abandon another human being and possibly kill them by accident because I didn't take them with me.

Five of my friends who turned up [at the I–10/I–610 interchange] had been in the Convention Center. They had an easier time of it than my friend who escaped. They had put an old lady and a cripple in a shopping cart and pushed them across the bridge to Gretna because that was supposed to be safe. When they got there, [someone] took the old lady and the cripple and sent them to the hospital. Then they said, "Get on this bus, and we will evacuate you."

So we all end up in Kenner. There were piles of garbage as tall as I am. People were shitting everywhere because there were no toilets. There was no anything. We figured out that between the eight of us, we had about fifteen hundred dollars cash. Most of us had taken money out thinking we were going to pay rent on the first, which didn't happen. We found everyone we could with a car, cops, firemen, Red Cross volunteers, news crews. We found like five news crews. We said, "Look, we've got money, and we've got pictures from inside the Convention Center from before they let the media in there. We'll give it to you if you help us get out. Please take us to La

Place."

Everyone said, "No. We have things to do. We have appointments to keep," they said. Blah, blah, blah. I'm like, that's really great. I just buried my friend in a park. Drive us out of here, you assholes! No one would do it. No one would help us.

So no one would help, we weren't getting anything done, and we were looking more and more suspicious; eight white people with piercings, tattoos and strange hair sitting in a circle off from the rest of the group. It was really time to move on.

Saturday morning, at about five a.m., we got up. We waited until no one was paying attention, and we found a hole in the fence. We yanked the hole open so we could all fit, found a shopping cart on the side of the road, and put everything that belonged to eight people and two cats in cat carriers into the shopping cart. It all fit. We started walking down the interstate. Nobody knew how far La Place was.

Why La Place?

Because we heard they had power. We saw a giant police barricade about a half mile up. We knew we were not going to get through it. We figured they were going to beat our asses and take us right back to where we started. We had to think of something fast. We saw this news crew talking to a homeless man, so we ran over. The news crew was so excited to see us. They totally shooed the bum away and started to talk to us. We were eight punk-rock kids with tattoos and flame-colored hair pushing a shopping cart down the I-10, so they were very excited. It was *Dateline*.

We were thinking, "The cops are seeing us talking to the news. Now if they kick our asses and try to take us back to that scary camp, the news will film it, and they will have to stop." Or something like that. I don't know. We were all delirious. Have I mentioned we hadn't slept in two days at that point? We stayed awake all night. No one could sleep with helicopters going over us every five minutes, lighting up the whole place like friggin' Christmas.

What kind of questions did they ask you?

They asked us where we were coming from, and we told them. We told them how terrible it was, and that they should run right over there and expose it to the world. We were thinking that if we get on TV, our families might see us. They might know we were alive. Then the reporter pulled out her cell phone. The first person to take the phone was Megan. She started bawling. She was on the phone with her father, saying, "Please come pick us up. I know it will take you 14 hours to get here, but that will probably be how long its going to take us to walk, so could you please pick us up in La Place?" Then we all started crying because she was crying. [At the same time] we were thinking to ourselves, all they're going to show is her crying, which was exactly what happened. Two days later, after it was all said and done, we watched *Dateline*, and it was five minutes of Megan crying. But our families saw us on TV. Double bonus points for that one. Word got around that we were alive. Then we said, "Hey guys, could you give us a ride?" "No," they said, "we have to go do whatever now." They were all the same, I swear to God. They were very excited about capitalizing on our suffering, and then they left. But at least the cops couldn't beat us. We walked right past them.

We got [to LaPlace] at about three in the afternoon. When we got to the bridge, there was this guy who was very nice. He was this crazy, Creole swamp guy. He had been in Vietnam, and he was a little cracked. He loaded us up in the back of his truck and started racing at 120 miles an hour down the bridge. He was trying to free us from the Hurricane or something. He almost killed us when he swerved to avoid a family of baby ducks that were trying to cross the road. I was thinking to myself, "I remember the day I moved [to New Orleans]. I drove down the same bridge, and it was about noon. It was really hot, and the air in my tires expanded. I got a flat on this bridge." Just then, his tire goes out. When was it going to end? We all got out of the truck. We got Megan to go out and hold the sign that said we needed a lug wrench. We had a spare tire that turned out to be older than Moses, and we had a lug wrench that wasn't the right size. Everything that could possibly be wrong with this situation was wrong. We were holding the sign, and no one was passing. There was no traffic. There were no cars, and it was hot. We were only out there for about half an hour though. Before you know it, here was some crazy asshole going backwards on the side of the interstate at about 70. He was hauling ass towards us. We had to jump out of the way back in the bed of the truck. The guy stopped, jumped out of the car with an AR-14, a .44 Magnum and an Uzi, which he shoved into our faces. He had a gun strapped to his back and a gun in each hand. He said, "I don't have any food or water." It was like summer camp with machine guns, and I was thinking, "This crazy motherfucker is going to shoot us all. This is great." Then he said, "I was just saying that I didn't have anything because I didn't want you to rob me. Do you need any help?"

The guy got the lug wrench and started changing the tire. Every five minutes, he was going back to the car and getting another gun. He had amassed this pile of guns and he had them sitting on top of the popped tire. [When he was finished], he came over and said, "You see this? This is why I don't get any of those crazy tattoos." He had shark bite scars all over his arms.

It was just getting weirder and weirder by the second, but he did change our tire. Then he said, "I'll escort you guys to Baton Rouge." We were like, "Oh no, that's OK." Then he called all the girls over and said, "Here, drink this." I thought, "I'm not even gonna argue with the guy at this point." So I drank out of the mystery jug. It tasted like orange juice and rum. Then he said, "You ever shot one of these?" He held up an Uzi. "No, sir, we've never shot an Uzi," I said. "Well, try it," he said.

So I shot the Uzi. The cops pull up a second later. The guy went over to the cop car and leaned into the window for about five seconds. Then the cop pulled off and drove away. I don't know what he said to him. We were done with this guy by then. Everybody piled into the truck. We were pulling away when I looked behind the trees I had been shooting at. I saw houses. I had been firing a fucking Uzi into a residential neighborhood for the last ten minutes.

What have you learned, if anything, from this experience?

Growing up, I always had this kind of robots-will-take-over-the-world, Mad Max, post-apocalyptic wet dream. I always thought that would be really cool, and that I would make it out on top if that ever happened. It kind of did happen, and I'm proud of myself. The most distressing thing I saw—I mean, I've seen dead bodies before, and it's not like I've lived in some sheltered neighborhood my whole life—was when we were walking around the city going on food missions. When all the looting was going on, we saw this boutique clothing store. It's called Frock Candy, and it's on Magazine Street. It looked like no one had been in there, until I noticed that there was this bottom panel of glass missing. Out of the bottom climbed this girl, not a day over fourteen. She climbed out with an armful of nice blouses. She smiled at me just like she would smile if I passed her on her way to church. It sunk in right then and there that people are fucking horrible. We're opportunistic, and we're monsters. We're always jumping to capitalize when something bad happens. And that was exactly what people did.

In the Same Financial Boat

Michelle Balot
In Her Own Words

Michelle Balot grew up in uptown New Orleans and had always accepted hurricanes and hurricane warnings as part of life. She sensed, however, that Katrina was a serious threat and convinced her husband to evacuate with their children. She expresses her devastation and exhaustion as she attempts to move on.

I felt I had reason to be concerned about this storm since just a few weeks before the warnings, I suffered an enormous loss. My godfather died, and I was having a terrible time coping. I was just working through feelings of despair and desperation when I heard about Katrina's path. Despite all that, for the first time in weeks, I felt that my life was going well. My daughter was receiving ongoing treatment for autism and making some progress. I was starting (and loving) graduate school at UNO, and my husband William and I were actually getting along well for a change. We were in our own home for the first time in the past three years of our marriage. Plus, we finally found a church where we could worship freely with our children. The last thing I needed was a threat from a major hurricane.

As Katrina whirled in the Gulf, drifting closer to the Big Easy, residents frantically prepared their homes and geared up with supplies: water, non-perishables, and a three-day supply of essentials. Some chose to stay for various reasons, many expecting it not to be that bad, and others, having evacuated before, perhaps were not willing to sacrifice their peace of mind for hours of bumper-to-bumper traffic in sweltering heat. Then, of course, there were those without a choice, those who could not afford to leave, who didn't have transportation, or who were too ill to be moved. My family and I fell in the category of people whose finances stood between potential safety and eminent danger. Like many families in the city, we lived from paycheck to paycheck, carefully counting every dollar to cover our long list of expenses. The single paycheck earned by my husband was barely enough to pay our living expenses and debts, so we received food stamps from the state government in order to eat.

As the storm approached, I prayed for God to spare us, just one more time, please. Although my husband just got paid on Friday, we were broke by Saturday because there were so many bills to pay. Once we paid the electric bill, we were left with approximately 63 dollars. Our car needed a tune up, the tread on our tires was low, and our brakes were bad. Originally, William said that we should just pack up the car and head out of town, but the car was not safe enough to take the children. Honestly, he seemed unmoved by the storm, which was not unusual for him, since William never worries about such things. In fact, each year he would poke fun at me for tracking tropical systems and gathering supplies. This time, because of our money troubles, he decided that we were going to wait out the storm. I could not imagine another alternative, so I anxiously did what he said. For the next few hours, as Katrina drew nearer, I realized that this idea was absurd. There was no way we could wait out a hurricane with two small children, including one with special needs. In case of emergency, where would we go? What if we ran out of food and water? As time passed, I grew increasingly uneasy to the point that I had diarrhea.

Throughout the day, I spoke to my sisters, and we all seemed to be in the same financial boat. Miraculously, my oldest sister, Charlotte, was able to convince her employer to lend her a bus to get our entire family to higher ground. William did not want to evacuate on the bus because he felt like he would not be in charge of the decisions. Plus, he looked forward to taking a road trip, which I thought was a stupid idea to have in this time of emergency. I did not share this thought with him, of course. We argued for hours about the decision to take the bus, and William threatened to stay in the city alone. I was frantic at this suggestion, but this did not prevent him from angrily throwing our suitcases in the car and yelling for my mother to come downstairs, so he could bring us to the bus. I cried and begged him to change his mind, arguing that this was no time for him to be selfish, and that he had two small children to consider. We argued until we finally agreed to leave our car and take the stupid bus.

On the bus, I imagined this evacuation being portrayed as a *Lifetime* movie. I called it "Katrina: The Story of Survival." I looked out the window at cars of people passing by, some jam-packed and some with a sole passenger. Each car was headed to an unknown fate. I wondered about the people who were left in the city, not so much about those who were determined to stay for their own personal reasons, but those who wanted to leave but had no choice in the matter. I worried because I knew that feeling. I remembered having to stay in the city during the threat of a major storm because I lacked the transportation and money to get out of town. It's a desperate and frightening feeling.

In all honesty, this trip we were on was scary, too. I felt that our fate was as uncertain as the people in the city, and we had much to lose as well. Nevertheless, this was our destiny, a bus headed north of Louisiana and hoping to get there safely. When we arrived, we were in Jackson, Mississippi. My sister, the driver, made an unfortunate decision. Frustrated by the bickering of the sixty New Orleanians whose safety she was coincidentally responsible for, she stopped the bus and looked for the safest place for her passengers to lodge. The search ended at the Mississippi Coliseum in a Red Cross Shelter.

While I waited in the shelter, I heard the media increasingly refer to evacuees as refugees. Eventually, I started using the same terminology, not realizing the negative connotations. I wondered, "Well, aren't we seeking refuge?" It was not until I heard former New Orleans Mayor Morial refute the term on *Meet the Press* that it became clear. He said, "These are not refugees. They are American citizens!" Unfortunately the experiences of many of the survivors of Katrina left them feeling like refugees. The truth is that while those of us who evacuated to other states were American citizens, some of us were not treated as such. I never knew that there were such strong cultural divides between the cities and states in the United States that caused people to view evacuees as outsiders.

While I was in the shelter, I found myself contemplating people's predicaments and considering their circumstances. I wondered how so many people got to the shelter and if any of them lost loved ones. I thought about why certain people slept close together and others, like my family, separated themselves by their few possessions. I felt like a fool for looking at the situation through a sociological lens, but this was how I coped, by separating myself from what was happening and by studying everything and everyone around me.

I felt like a prisoner in that shelter. We were allowed to leave, but once inside, the volunteers watched us closely. Eventually they traded places with members of the state police, who kept a close watch on our activities. Announcements were made frequently cluing us into meal times and other scheduled tasks, such as the doctor's hours. It was loud, cold, and dirty. The children played all day while the adults worried; some people sat outside all day, while others slept the time away. I spent most of my time keeping close watch over my daughters. In fact, I actually locked them into their strollers for hours at a time because I was worried about them getting lost or kidnapped. I stayed inside for the entire week and only ventured out to take a shower in the shelter across the street.

Finally, the purple wrist bands appeared. A white male volunteer told us to wear them because the bands would keep track of how many meals were needed and determine who was supposed to be in this particular shelter, but we felt violated. The adults bickered, while the children made fun of their "prison bands." Of course it didn't help to have armed guards watching us all day and night, but the incessant announcements and jail-like wrist bands made it even more degrading. I knew that certain security measures had to be taken, but they did so at the cost of our already shaken morale.

After a week, we held a family meeting. My sisters, mom, aunts, uncles, cousins, husband, and I, who had been together throughout this journey, would now have to go our separate ways. The shelter where we found protection was no longer a safe haven for us, so we all agreed to locate friends or relatives in other places where we could go until the situation improved. Those who could not find a place to go went to a shelter run by a local church. My husband contacted his relatives, who live in the suburbs about an hour from Philadelphia, Pennsylvania. They offered for us to stay in their home once they heard that the levees broke. They sounded really nice on the phone. I had only met them once at my wedding six years ago. But once we got there, they starting acting quite distant toward us. We eventually found a temporary apartment because we didn't want to be a burden on them or cause any conflicts in their marriage. Since then, I have seen them twice, and each time has been pretty uncomfortable.

This has been an exhausting experience. Sometimes I feel totally defeated. For weeks I was so fatigued that I was too tired to be angry. I generally feel sad, lonely, and disgusted. Maybe that's part of the stages of grief, so it all may have been very normal. Still, it was much to bear. Even now my chest hurts, my head hurts, and I have painful tingles all over my body. I feel like I want to throw up most of the time. Most of all, I feel helpless, which is the worst part of it. Plus, the distance from my family adds to this terrible sense. Sometimes I want to cry, but I keep trying to be strong in front of Will and the children. I figure things are hard enough as they are, and I don't want to add to anyone else's frustrations. Lying down doesn't make it feel much better, but at least if I cry in bed it's OK because it's only me.

What usually keeps me going is my schoolwork, but I have lost my passion for that right now. I feel like I have to defend my choices to everyone. Why should I stay away from home if there is no damage? Why should I be depressed if I didn't lose anything? But everything that I know is gone. The house that I grew up in was sold a few months ago. All of my childhood pictures, papers, and report cards that my mother saved for the past thirty years have been destroyed. I feel like my heritage is lost. I feel like I am lost, and I don't know how to begin to find myself, so that I can heal. It hurts so much, and at the same time it seems unreal. I wonder, "What did I do wrong, and what do I do now? How long am I going to feel this way?"

And then there is the anger. The unprecedented, unintelligible, indescribable rage that boils inside me. It showed up one day. It was probably something minute that set it off, the never-ending pile of dishes, or the clothes that keep piling up on the sofa of our rented apartment. Whatever it was, it set off an explosion inside me that is slowly burning away. I have a dire urge to release this rage, but no reasonable outlet to do so, so it festers and gnaws at me slowly and painfully. I often wonder what I have to look forward to now.

One of the hardest things for me, besides deciding whether to return to New Orleans, has been making everyday decisions. Simple things, like what I feel like eating for dinner, have stressed me out so much in the past few weeks. It just seems like too much to bear. There are too many decisions to make at once, and no matter what we decide, whether to return or stay put, whether to rebuild or start over somewhere else, all of these choices will affect us for the rest of our lives and change us in some way. I have been dreaming about the disaster every night since the storm hit. I dream of hurricanes, tornadoes, wars, and family conflicts. Now it's at the point that I do not to go to sleep.

My family all evacuated together and survived the shelters in Mississippi together. Now we are scattered throughout the United States with our closest means of contact being our cell phones. It is very hard for me to deal with being in a strange place, but even more so because my family is so displaced. What makes the situation harder is that most of us have lost everything. While my house is one of the only two still habitable, I still feel a great loss. My mother continues to say, "At least we didn't lose anyone," but I feel like from the time I set foot on that bus, I lost a sense of myself.

I lost my identity in the shelter in Mississippi, and in our relatives' home in Pennsylvania. I wonder who I am and what my purpose is, if not to fill some place in the spectrum of what is/was my family.

Those things I used to love and enjoy are part of a distant memory now. Now it's time for a new beginning and a fresh start. It's time to start a new life that is not only laden with possibilities, but also branded by loss. It's a shame, but it's a reality; life must go on.

It Was a Very Peculiar Time

John T. Martin
As Told to Nicole Pugh

John T. Martin's business card reads "Spiritual Services: Readings, Rituals, and Gris-Gris." He is the manager of the Voodoo Museum on Dumaine Street, in the French Quarter. He lingered for a few days after Katrina then packed his menagerie of exotic pets and headed for Baton Rouge.

Before the storm, things were pretty much the status quo. Everybody was getting ready for Labor Day weekend, which is a pretty prominent weekend here in the Quarter. I think the reason a lot of people stayed was because they had heard the weather men cry wolf so many times. At the last minute, things seemed to take a turn, but [people] just couldn't take it seriously because of the negativity that the press always attached to impending disasters in the past. For Hurricane Ivan, we didn't even have a drop of rain.

This was a very peculiar time. I knew that something was out of the ordinary when the animals that I have upstairs, the exotics that would be more pure of nature, went into hiding two days before. My big iguana hid in the cabinet in the bathroom. My python hid behind the couch. Nobody wanted to be close to the windows. Of course, the day before the storm, all the birds left. It gave you this idea that something very, very serious was going to happen. The day of the storm, there were heavy winds, and it started getting a bit scary. There was a lot of debris, a lot of chimneys coming off of places here in the Quarter, a lot of copper sheeting. It was very dangerous to be outside. There was a neighbor here that had a brand new Mercedes. He left it parked on the street. [The wind] picked up a two-by-four and ran it completely through his back window and out the front. The building shook on occasion. I wound up having to put things down in my front living room because there were two leaks there and also one in the bedroom. My neighbor in the back, Christy, from New York, was very freaked. I had her come over into the main house because it was a lot more stable than the other.

We finally made it through, and Christy and I went out to look at things. We went out by [Jackson] Square and the back of the Cathedral garden. Two huge trees had fallen and left Jesus standing minus two fingers. The birds that did stay were very visibly shaken. I remember this little sparrow trying to come to us in Pirate's Alley. He wouldn't let us take him, but he would come close. He wanted help.

It was like everything fell apart. You had these rumors as to what was being done with the levees, that they were going to blow up one to even up things and that there would be ten feet of water in the Quarter. That had everybody really upset. Also, the fact that we couldn't get any responsible media. Nobody knew what was happening. Of course, we could see at the end of the street here on Dumaine that North Rampart was filling with water. The lower end of St. Ann also had water.

In the afternoon [on Tuesday], I was sitting at the 905 Royal Hotel with the two ladies who owned it. We saw a group of Goth kids coming up the road with an entire rack they had stolen out of a store. The police stopped them for about one minute and then let them go. We mentioned to each other, "If this is how it is going to go, it is just opening up the door for anybody to do anything they want to do." My neighbor and I toured the neighborhood in his SUV. They were breaking into grocery stores. They were breaking into Wal-Mart. The police were doing this as well, carrying out big items.

It made you know that you could not trust the police.

We loaded up my neighbor's SUV with the big 300-pound python, Eugene, along with three other snakes, two lizards and four birds. Eugene's so big; he's never been in a cage in his life. He was loose with us in the truck. We made it up to the end of Royal by the Model Inn, and there was water on the road. Then we crossed over to Poydras, and again there was water on the road. We headed towards Tchoupitoulas to get onto the bridge. We were crossing over Poydras, and there were two dead bodies on the sidewalk. As we got over to the other side, three black men started coming towards the van. I mentioned to my neighbor, "Gamble, these guys are going to try to carjack us, and we are going to have to run over them." They got close enough to see me, and the 300-pound python, and they changed their minds. We got up onto the bridge and could see that there was looting going on in the Wal-Mart. Going up to the bridge, there were law enforcement people with machine guns keeping other people from going across. Part of the reason was that [someone] had already torched the local mall. The law enforcement were putting a stop to this, even though it imperiled a lot of innocent people.

We didn't get [to Baton Rouge] until nine o'clock at night. Normally, it takes fifty minutes. It was a nice, quiet neighborhood and, of course, the animals felt like they were totally safe there. The big one, he's been to the house before. He came in and surveyed everything and went over and curled up by this big palm tree in the corner of the dining room. He lay there for three days. Everybody there was very intrigued with the animals. All the neighborhood kids had to come over and visit. We made the most of it. Baton Rouge is a far cry from New Orleans, culturally or otherwise. It was a hard five weeks.

Here in the Quarter, everybody looks out after each other. They tried to hold things together as long as they could. We could not depend on the local police. We could not depend on the mayor. We could not depend on the governor. The only semblance of peace came when the military came. Actually, when I came back, which was October the 3rd, it gave me peace that the military was still here and that they were patrolling the streets at night because I have no faith in the local police department. I have no faith in the powers that be. Our councilwoman, who has been very vocal in the past, did not make so much as an appearance. Then all of a sudden, she diverted her attention to Algiers, where she lives. The mayor, I think he's still living in a fog. I don't think he thinks he did as bad a job as he did. If I was in his position, I [wouldn't be able to] sleep at night, knowing that I had that many deaths on my plate. They could have easily asked for volunteers and used the transit buses to get people out. They didn't. Amtrak offered a train. They turned that down. I don't think that they were thinking.

In general, though, I think it was grossly mishandled. The cop-out of saying the governor was overly emotional because she's a woman, I think that is the most ridiculous thing I've ever heard. I have heard of some very organized women. The mayor of Galveston is a good example. She stepped up to the plate and went over the edge as far as her duties were concerned. She was there for the entire time. She made sure that her people were taken care of before she was taken care of. And when a person accepts that responsibility, that's what it's about. I even question whether saying that having the pump operators evacuate was the right thing to do. I think that there are certain positions that, when you take them, that's part of the position. The same way with the police who were hired to protect and serve. They were neither protecting nor serving. As far as the pump people were concerned, they were in a life-or-death situation. You have to make up your mind. Is it better to give up one life or give up a hundred? When you have the ability to save those people, and you have taken on that position, then that should come first.

[When we came back,] everybody gave each other a big hug, and I think everybody had their cry. I think anybody that said they didn't is lying. It's still a trying time. I've seen a lot of my dear friends go out of business. And I'll venture to say that a lot more will go out of business before this is all over. And I question if it will be over. We have committees up the yang, but I don't see anybody doing anything viable to keep this from happening again. Yet the hurricane season is only six months off, and it is supposed to be more intense over the next five years. We did not get a direct hit. What if we would have? This may not be the storm that we have always feared. That may be the one to come.

I've been through three storms. I don't think I'll go through another one. It makes you realize the importance of family, of close friends. The material things are just not important. They can be taken away as easily as they are earned. No one should set their stock in material means.

My time is not that far off. I probably won't make it to the next hurricane season. I've had a tumor for several years, but it has started to grow. I think God takes care of you in strange ways. In the course of riding everything out in Baton Rouge, I was approached by Marathon Oil on a piece of property that I did not even realize that I had. I sold it. It is my money, not the government's money. And it happened at the right time. I do think that God takes care of you. You have to remember that the very reason why God gives you today is the very reason why it is called the *present*. He might not give it to you tomorrow. So you do what you should do today. If you need to make peace, make peace. Only you know whether you need to or not.

Even the Crow on the Roof is Smiling

James Andrew Busenlener
As Told to Sylvia Schneller

James Andrew Busenlener, age five, tells the story of his family's evacuation and discusses the changes in the city after the storm.

This story is about a Hurricane named Katrina, and about a family whose house got struck by the hurricane. In the family are Mama Tanya, Daddy Jim, Andrew, Ashley, and Mattie. The family left their house so the hurricane couldn't hit them. They went to Houston. I didn't want to leave my house and go to Houston because I liked my house.

This is my house before the hurricane:

Then the hurricane hit. It was night and very black and very scary. If my family had stayed in their house, the hurricane would have sucked them up. Then my belly and my back would have gotten hurt. Some houses were sucked up by the hurricane but not my house. It didn't get sucked up because it was made of wood. One window got broken. Although nothing else happened to my house, a big tree branch fell and broke my swing set. My mommy and daddy told me some of my neighbors' houses flooded, but mine didn't. I was glad my house didn't flood because my toys would have washed away.

This is my house during the hurricane with the black hurricane sucking up other people's houses

I stayed with my cousins while the hurricane was happening. I liked it there and wasn't scared because we stayed in the upstairs and had nice toys to play with.

After the hurricane we went home. Some things were different. TCBY wasn't open. We couldn't go to our school because the hurricane broke it. I went to another school, but I don't remember where it was. In Houston, I went to Alexander, my cousin's school. I liked it because on Fridays I got to pick a toy.

This is my school now with me and my school bag. I have a happy face because I am back. Even the crow on the roof is smiling because he likes Trinity, too.

I was glad to go home again because I could play with my stuffed animals.

The End.

I'm Not Interested in Talking

New Orleans Police Officer
Interviewed by Matthew Peters

New Orleans Police Officers were forbidden to speak on the record about their Hurricane Katrina experiences without written permission from their supervisors. This officer worked twelve-hour shifts, seven days a week, from August 29 to October 1, 2005. Then he was allowed to work twelve hours a day, five days a week.

I'm not interested in talking about what I saw, or about what I've had to do, to anyone. Ever.

The City Wasn't Prepared

Dwight Robinette, Jr.
Interviewed by Sheila Willis

Dwight Robinette, Jr. has been a Louisiana State Police officer for over ten years. He has worked in drug enforcement and hostage negotiations, among other duties. Robinette served on the Search and Rescue Unit and later the Search and Recovery Unit after Katrina.

Have you ever witnessed a disaster of this nature before?

No.

Were you properly trained for a situation of this nature?

No.

What was your involvement in the preparation for this storm?

Basically for the preparation, State Police's duty is to provide protection and prevention in the life… we more or less help in the life and property of Louisianans. Prior to Katrina, just like in any other disaster, it's our duty to assist with the evacuation, and the preparation for any natural disasters. This is a yearly thing that we do during every hurricane season […] Never in a million years would I have thought I would've, you know, seen and done the things that I did in this past year.

What was your first reaction when you realized how serious the storm was?

Just like anyone else… My first priority was to get my family out. Make sure they were evacuated; make sure they were safe. I tried to preserve or save what I could which…it didn't help. No one thought the water would be as high as it was, the disaster, the devastation would be as extreme as it was. We were all sent up here to headquarters, or everyone that was in that general area of the eye of the storm, should I say, and that would be the

Troop B area, part of Troop A, and part of Troop L area. We all were housed up here until that Monday around noon, at which time, it came from our superintendent, Col. Whitehorn, and brought down the rest of our various command staff, at which time were dispatched back into New Orleans to assist with, you know, search and rescue, and various other duties that were tasked upon us.

So the search and rescue started?

It actually started Monday.

Prior to the storm?

Yes

And what did you do the first day after the storm hit?

Well, it wasn't a lot that we could do. We came down, and part of my job was to go out and analyze, do an analysis of the areas where we could travel, what roadways were open, and which roadways were closed, to get intelligence and bring it back to Troop B command, to advise which routes troopers could take so that we wouldn't lose any vehicles, or put anyone in harm's way. At that point and time, there were various agencies from all over the United States. The calls were sent out for assistance. Various State Police Departments, Sheriff's Departments, other municipalities, and everyone met at a centralized location and at that time, a plan was formulated to take sectors of the city, more or less, and go out and start looking for people.

What part of the city did you work? Did you work one particular area?

We were scattered throughout the area. Everywhere. In the beginning, it was more fanning out and then just helping people, and there were people who were at the Superdome and Convention Center, and every street you could think of. You know, you'd be driving or in a boat, going along, and you'd stumble across someone that needed to be evacuated. The Coast

Guard, Aviation Fleet…New Mexico, California, I mean, that's just some of the states I can think of that sent helicopters and rescue planes and stuff down.

You were involved in the rescue at the Superdome?

I was initially not, I was, I more or less provided security for some of our upper staff command to go in and evaluate, and then do an analysis of what was going on in the Superdome. I was part of a protection team at that time, or small tactical element, more or less. Myself and a couple of DEA agents, we provided a little security, like I said, for some of, you know, the higher rank.

In your opinion, how serious were the problems at the Superdome?

Extreme. Very extreme.

Can you elaborate on that, or not really?

The city wasn't prepared for the amount of people that sought shelter at the Dome. For one, electricity was out. To my understanding, within the first two days, they were out of water; a lot of people were out of food. I witnessed bodies, I witnessed some sights that I care not to, you know, to describe for various reasons. It was, it was inhumane, the conditions. People weren't prepared; they didn't take the evacuation notice seriously. They more or less took essentials, and I'm not even going to say essentials. They took things that were not essential, televisions, radios. Instead of clothing and food, they were bringing personal belongings.

Were these people who had no transportation, or did they just refuse to leave their homes?

I think it was half and half. I'd say a majority were those that didn't have transportation, or didn't have an opportunity to leave due to maybe financial matters. Maybe some were physical, some were medical. I think a vast amount of it was just stubbornness. How many times over the past couple of years we've played wolf, or cried wolf. Every time hurricane season comes along, the average person leaves for a day or two, spends upwards of $500 to $1000, to evacuate, gas, food and shelter, and come back and then they realize that now you've put yourself in a financial hole or a burden because you evacuated and nothing happened. And I think they took things lightly this time again, and when they did realize the severity of the storm, it was a little too late. And the roadways had been shut down, and the storm was upon us, so all higher ground or shelter that they could seek was the Superdome or the Convention Center.

How long did your unit continue to rescue people or was your unit involved in the rescue?

Search and Rescue ran all the way through, I'd say into November. It ran all the way into November, at which time it changed more or less into Search and Recovery. Search and Recovery kind of started also up in the latter part of September, early part of October, and when we say search and recovery, a lot of people were looking for missing loved ones, and that's where the problem came into effect with that situation, so, even up to this date and time, they are still working on looking for missing people.

What kind of response did you receive from the rescuees during your efforts to save their lives?

It was mixed […] I'd say the majority was looking to be rescued, taken to higher ground. A percentage was looking for food and water, and they wanted to stay where they were at, and a very small percentage was pretty much annoyed or deterred from our presence, and those were the people that just, for whatever reason, don't like the police. Some people were mentally and emotionally stressed from everything that was, you know, they were trying to take everything in at one time, and a lot of people couldn't deal with it. I think it caused them to, more or less, have an emotional rollercoaster. They didn't know really how to act, or which direction to go, so they were looking for some direction and some form of leadership.

And would you say the people that wanted to stay, that refused to leave, were they elderly people?

Majority were, yes, I'd say 90% of those that decided to stay were elderly. A lot of people, their roots lie within New Orleans, born and raised, families, and decades of families and generations, should I say, they didn't have anything else. Their property was their livelihood.

Did any of the rescuees that you assisted, did they indicate where they were planning to evacuate to?

At that point and time they didn't have a choice. It depended where you evacuated from, and who you were evacuated by. The Coast Guard, in the initial phase of it, used I-10 by Causeway, as more of a drop-off shelter. From the Convention Center, a lot of people were being air-lifted and dropped there, and buses were moving people out. From what I understand, I know people were being sent to Houston, to Dallas, to New York, Chicago, Michigan. I've even heard of people being taken to Canada, so there were a lot of places throughout the United States that were set up as shelters, evacuation shelters where they were taking evacuees.

How many officers were in each unit? Was there more than one unit?

Oh, several. There were several, yeah, yeah, I couldn't even tell you how many exactly. We had a platoon of officers, like I said, Sheriff's Office, Police Departments, State Police, and I don't want to leave anybody out, I mean, it was what, California, Michigan, Virginia, New Mexico, Texas, Tennessee, Ohio, New York, New Jersey, Oklahoma. I mean, that, that's the ones that I can remember working with. Mississippi sent down some of their people, and there was a lot of, a lot of different agencies, and you had, I mean just the various groups, you had a 24-hour shift role, and at any point in time you could have anywhere up to several hundred people out, anywhere from a four to a ten-man unit, depends on the number of boats, depending on the number of helicopters, depending on the number of vehicles that were able to travel and get to designated areas.

Each of these police officers that came from another state to assist, were you all assigned to the Search and Rescue?

Yes, they came, and they had different functions. Initially, it was everyone came in for the fact of search and rescue. Some came into provide security, to assist with patrols, to assist with checkpoints for the Interstate. It was like I said. It was several other areas of need or assistance that were rendered. The primary one was to go in and rescue.

And if someone was injured, what was the protocol for that?

The military came in, and they set up evac. They set up medvac. They set up a lot of different units. They were stationed throughout the city anywhere from the Westbank, Convention Center, Superdome, at various points of the Interstate, and anyone that needed medical attention was sent to one of those. They set one up for us. We were all given hepatitis shots, tetanus shots, and received any needed medical assistance. I know to this date we didn't lose one Trooper due to injuries or leaving the job, anything like that.

At what point did it stop being rescue and become recovery?

The flood waters went, I think it was the second week of September, it was about six, seven weeks exactly, that the lower Ninth Ward was the last area to drain, and I would stretch it maybe as far as to eight weeks. So you are talking maybe the third week of September, when all the flood waters were down, and everyone was able to get in and really do a true evaluation of the situation. And prior to that, we were using boats to get to houses and cut holes in roofs, and then go in the attics and search for people. Our fundamental role was to go out into the area and look for bod... look for people who needed assistance. Once we hit those areas, then, of course, the calls started pouring in, the 911 calls. People being trapped, people looking for their loved ones, or people looking for their animals. Not only did we look for humans, we also rescued animals. I would say, the beginning of October was probably your true time for search and recovery.

What would you say the casualty rate was in that recovery period?

The numbers that they're giving is somewhere between, I think, 1200 and 1500 or 1600. I've only observed myself, probably close to ten […] I can't account for the rest of the units. I'm only going on numbers that the city provided, or that the census provided. Do I think it's true? No.

It's higher?

Oh, it's higher, definitely higher. Definitely higher. Like I said, there are things that I observed and have knowledge of that, and I'm not obligated to dwell upon, that I know, that would push it higher.

How would you say you are personally coping with this disaster?

Being a person of sound mind and strong morals and a strong mental capacity, I did pretty good. I lost a grandmother [pause] in the hurricane. My family was despondent. Everybody is pretty much, they're all scattered throughout the United States now.

Your family has evacuated to different states?

Yes, Michigan, Texas, you name it, they're there. The first, the first two days was hard. I couldn't find my brother. He's a New Orleans Police Officer, and we lost communication during the storm, so I spent, besides rescuing people, I spent my first two days looking for him, and I found him, and it made things a little easier. That Friday was when I found out that my grandmother had drowned […] I had to go in and, you know, recover her body.

Where did your grandmother live?

She was in a nursing home. They had told us that they had evacuated everyone. But it turned out that she wanted to stay with her friends down in the nursing home, you know. I think she was 78. No, I'm sorry, 82. She was fairly, you know, medically decent for a person [who is] 82. She had her right mind and everything. She lost her husband about six years ago, and she's been done a while. She has all of us family that provide love and support for her, but, just like a lot of people, she decided she wanted to stay, and it was her will to stay. So, they didn't evacuate her like they said they did.

So all of the people stayed in the nursing home?

They started evacuating people right after the storm hit. The water came in, and they moved everyone from the first level to the second floor. They put approximately sixty or more elderly people in a small second-story room. I got the call Friday morning, and myself and another Trooper, a friend of mine, we made our way down to the nursing home. We had to go through a lot of the water. That area was pretty bad at that point in time. There were still small, I would say gangs, or bands of people who were scavenging their way through the city. They were burning and looting and shooting, and things of that nature, so we, it was like a little special mission, he and I set on the road to find her, and when I found her body, it was at that time, 11:00 a.m.; [she] had died from heat exhaustion. She was one of them. I think totally, they probably, I don't know exactly, I think about 20 elderly died as a result of the heat.

And you have a son, correct?

Yes.

Where did he evacuate to?

Michigan.

Is he still there?

He's still there. He's in school. He's doing well.

And how old is your son?

Nine.

On a personal note, can you tell me how your life has changed since Katrina, and how has this storm affected you?

Katrina, just like anything else, there's good and bad to everything. The bad side, we'll go bad first, most of the time people go with good. The bad point is I no longer have a grandmother. I only have one living grandmother now. She's in Michigan. She left. She lost her home. My family has been relocated and disassembled. They are scattered all over, so we don't have that family unit, aunts, uncles, cousins. Everyone is all over the place.

Is your brother still in New Orleans?

My brother is in Destrehan, so he's a little closer. I lost all my worldly possessions, and I've lost all my son's baby pictures. I've lost every certificate that I've achieved through my training, and more or less all of your precious belongings. I lost a vehicle, lost all my clothing, so I was homeless for a while. It gave me another outlook on life. It gave me an opportunity to see how it might feel to be really in need. I was fortunate enough that I worked for a department that provided me assistance, food and shelter throughout the whole time, clothing, even gave me financial assistance later on. I had to purchase a new home. I was more fortunate than a lot of people because I was in a better situation to purchase, you know, a brand new home in a nice subdivision, purchased a new vehicle, and recently got engaged. I didn't think I'd get engaged again for a while.

The down side of it is that I'm separated from my son, and he lived with me, so I'm traveling back and forth to Michigan every month to see him, and it's a financial burden. That's the downfall of it. Part of the downfall is that I've taken on financial debt, per se, but the total outcome of it is that I've been able to get back on my feet. A lot of people are still in shelters. A lot of people still haven't been able to locate loved ones. A lot of people will not be able to recover, and that's the sad part of it. I thank God that I'm able to. I've been in a situation where I've been able to recover. Would I go through it again? No. I have a lot of people that look out for me and care about me. My Major for one. She brought me up here, transferred me up here to help me out, and things are looking better. They really are.

The sad side of it is that we're getting ready to start the process of the cycle all over again [with hurricane season around the corner]. There's a lot of animosity. There's a lot of fear, of course, to the unknown of what's going to occur in 2006. Throughout all the events that's transpired, and throughout the world, you know, the tsunamis, the mud slides, hurricanes, and forest fires, and you name it, you don't know what's in store for us. So I mean, I tell people all the time you have to have faith, you know, faith in God, and He has a purpose for all of us, and I try to be the best person I can be, and utilize my knowledge and my training, you know, to assist others. When I took the oath of office in 1995, it's what I took an oath of office to do, to protect and serve, and actually it came to that this past year. It was tested.

Something Terrible Was Happening

Peter Ward

As Told to Sylvia Schneller

Peter Ward's family evacuated to Dallas on Saturday as the storm approached. At the last minute, he decided to stay. Ward and his neighbor, a police officer, soon became involved in peace-keeping and search-and-rescue efforts throughout the city.

On Saturday morning, while watching television with friends, I realized the severity of Hurricane Katrina. Dr. Maestri was on, and he was talking about how vulnerable the city was to flooding. It recalled for me the number of times I'd escorted scientists through the marsh as they studied the effects of hurricanes on coastal erosion. For 15 years, I'd worked as a boat operator for the LSU Sea Grant Environmental Impact Group and remembered just how far inland the erosion was. In my gut, I knew we were going to experience severe flooding and damage. I told my wife we would have to evacuate. She is an artist, so she packed her paintings and our art collection. She gathered up our important papers and, in order to avoid traffic problems, left on Saturday for Dallas. I planned to follow her on Sunday after boarding up my house and raising things off the floor in my shop.

I didn't finish securing everything until 4:30 p.m. on Sunday. The weather was really bad, and I was concerned about driving. I was just leaving when my neighbor, a policeman, came over to my house to ask if he could borrow my deuce-and-a-half army truck. I have three, large, raised military vehicles that I use to haul the scraps and architectural salvage that I use in my business. He thought the truck might be useful if there was any flooding. I told him certainly he could have it, and as I was already concerned about driving anywhere with the weather being as bad as it was, I told him I'd accompany him in one of the other trucks and loan him the third one if he had someone who could drive it to police headquarters. He did, and the three of us went to his headquarters near Magazine Street and Louisiana

Avenue. We spent the night in a small brick and concrete pillbox near Touro Hospital. I felt safe there and hunkered down to await the storm's passage. At 5:30 a.m., I woke up to see the hurricane's full fury. A couple of policemen and I went outside. We stood between two buildings and watched as the air-conditioner unit blew off the roof of Touro Hospital. It fell to the street right in front of us and exploded into shreds. We would have been severely injured by the debris except that the pieces were immediately taken up by the wind and blown down the street. We estimated the wind to be blowing between 160 and 170 mph as it was funneled between the two buildings where we were standing. We decided it was too dangerous to be out and went inside.

When we got inside, everyone was listening to the police radio. An officer, who was trapped in his attic in New Orleans East, was calling for help. The storm surge had topped the levee there. He and his wife and two children had not evacuated and were now in their attic with the water rising rapidly; they were panicking. Many of the officers listening to him felt panicked also, and there was much chatter on the phone. No one was making any sense. Finally one of the officers told everyone to be quiet. He started talking calmly to the trapped policeman. He told him to look around the attic to see if he had any tools that he could use to chop a hole in the roof. When he replied in the negative, the policeman then asked if he had his gun with him. When he responded in the affirmative to that, he was told to take his gun, put it next to the roof, hold it close there, and shoot a hole in the roof. He was told to repeat that action over and over again, spacing the bullet holes one inch apart, until he had a hole big enough to climb through. We heard several shots, and then heard him say that his wife was holding the two children and that water was up to their neck. At that point the phone went dead. We were devastated thinking they had drowned. Later we found out that they had survived, that our sergeant's advice had saved him and his family. After the levees in New Orleans broke, we heard this story repeated thousands of times. We had a call for help at least every 15 minutes. It was awful. We felt helpless, as we were unable to get anywhere ourselves.

Shortly afterwards, the wind slackened enough so that we could safely go outside. The rain was still falling heavily, and there were some small areas of flooding uptown. Trees and tree limbs were down, which made it difficult to get around. It took us 45 minutes to reach Canal Street. Other than minor flooding and the debris, there was little else wrong. From 10:30 that morning until late in the afternoon, it was very quiet.

Around 5:30 that afternoon, the calls for help started coming in. We'd go out trying to investigate and see groups of stunned people everywhere. They looked at us as though saying, "What should we do?" We honestly didn't know what to tell them. Most often we told them to go to the Superdome. We attached trailers to the back of the trucks to pick up people and bring them to a dry street where they could then walk to the Superdome. We had few supplies at police headquarters, so on Monday evening, we found some cold red beans at Touro Hospital and ate that.

I was the first one in our group to drive down Napoleon Avenue after the storm. A couple of policemen and I were sent to Memorial hospital to pick up first-aid supplies. On Tuesday morning, while on one of these supply trips, I saw the most awesome thing. Right in front of me, a manhole cover blew out of the ground. A five foot geyser of water gushed out of it. Then along the street I saw the other manhole covers blowing off, all of them followed by a geyser of water. It was ominous. I didn't know the levees had broken but felt something terrible was happening. I couldn't imagine what was causing all this water under pressure to explode from the ground. Napoleon Avenue went from being bone dry to being covered by two feet of water within twenty minutes. I dropped one of the policemen off at the hospital and said I needed to hurry to get back closer to the river, or, in a few minutes, I wouldn't be able to make it. Three hours later, I made that same run and the water was four feet deep.

When I got back to the station house, the generator was on, and everyone was watching Mayor Nagin on the television saying that the levees had broken, and everyone needed to seek higher ground.

The water continued to come up on Tuesday night. People seeking dry ground were congregating. Some of the uptown gangs that had been fighting each other for years found themselves in closer proximity than usual. Around 2:30 a.m., gunfire broke out and continued for the next 48 hours. A lot of it sounded like it was coming from semi-automatic weapons. We attempted to make a run for the armory, but couldn't reach it because of the depth of the flood water. It seemed as though all hell broke loose. The criminal faction began looting the stores uptown. They stole not just food and water, but also guns and electronic equipment. The criminals had free run of the area. They simply opened the doors of houses and walked in taking what they wanted. They broke windows in stores and pharmacies. They took everything they could carry. We chased them down. If we caught them, we tried to talk them into putting the stuff back. Some did. If they put up a fight, we beat them up. We didn't shoot anyone. There was no place to take them or hold them. We did what we could to stop it.

At this point, everything is jumbled together. We took care of situations as they popped up in front of us. Driving around, we picked up people as we saw them and carried them to higher ground. People would hang on the outside of the truck. At times we had as many as 160 people in one truck. They were piled on top of one other. It was strange to see what they would try to save. Some had plastic bags with a few clothes in them; one had a lawn chair. So many were unprepared for what was happening. They were in their night clothes. One man had only a sheet on with a hole cut in the top for his head. We'd have a full truck, turn a corner, and see a mob of people who would run to the truck as soon as they saw us. Some of them had firearms; others had loot. Some refused to leave their loot behind in order to get into the truck.

I developed a route. It went from Tchoupitoulas Street to the I-10 to the Superdome. As I drove the route, I'd blow the horn. People would come running. The overpasses on the I-10 and the I-610 were islands for evacuees. Some people were so grateful that it broke my heart. Their thank you was so meaningful. Others were just the opposite. They were angry and demanding. Their complaining and arrogance made me angry.

On one such trip, I was asked to rescue a policeman from the flooded area on Claiborne Avenue just off the interstate. When I came off the overpass onto Claiborne, I saw a group of people looting three of the stores there. The water was very deep, but there was an eighty-by-thirty-foot island on the neutral ground that was dry. That was where they were storing the loot. I had no idea how they planned to get it out of there. That space was covered with electronic equipment, boxes of DVDs, and big-screen television sets. It was just getting dark, and when they saw the lights from my truck, they scattered into the water. There were eight or nine policemen in the back of my truck. By that time I'd seen so much looting that I was furious about it. I pulled up to the dry spot on the neutral ground just in front of the big screen television sets. I gunned my motor and ran right through the loot. I turned around and did it again. The policemen in the back of the truck were laughing. You should have seen the look on the looters' faces when the television sets exploded. It was as though they were saying, "I can't believe you've destroyed the things we've just stolen. How dare you?"

We came upon other crimes in progress. The policemen would try to run them down, but often were unsuccessful. On one occasion, we came upon one group of police breaking up the looting of a pharmacy. On the other side of the street was another group of officers berating those officers for finding an excuse to beat up on the "brothers." It was total mayhem. The few cars still left were being hijacked. There was continuous gunfire from the projects. The four-building compound on Napoleon and Magazine was under siege. The police were out-manned and out-armed.

Finally, on Tuesday night, a few members of the National Guard showed up. They had no rules of engagement and either no ammunition for their rifles or just two or three rounds. Some of them had just returned from Iraq and knew how to secure an area, so we posted some policemen at the gun stores to prevent the looting of more guns and ammunition and secured our station.

By Wednesday morning, the water had reached eight to ten feet in depth. The area we could drive through safely was very small. The streets around the Superdome flooded and people were moved to the Convention Center. The chaos there escalated with a crescendo-like force. I noticed that many at the Convention Center were like chameleons. When they got there, they looked stunned. Then they'd see a friend or family member or someone else like them. They'd speak for a few minutes with that person, and then join in with the looting or destruction. If a television reporter showed up with a camera, they'd immediately change their actions and appearance while on camera and, if given the chance, complain about their mistreatment. When the camera man turned away, they'd go back immediately to looting and destroying the Convention Center. I saw a man who seemed at first to appreciate the MRE he was given, then suddenly and angrily smash it against the wall of the Convention Center.

The acts of valor and of lawlessness by the members of the police department themselves were like the differences between Jesus and the Devil. Particularly outrageous was the alleged looting of Sewell Cadillac Company by police. I certainly saw a large number of policemen driving around in Cadillac and Escalante vehicles. It was said that they needed vehicles to do their job, but I know of a bunch that were never returned.

On Wednesday afternoon, I still had on the clothes I'd left my house wearing on Sunday. I hadn't had a bath. It was hot, and I stunk. So did the rest of the guys I was with. We saw a Kentwood truck parked on the street next to Touro. It was filled with water bottles. We took some, opened them, and filled up large buckets so we could bathe. I shaved and put on clean clothes. It was the best feeling. A grocery store owner in the neighborhood put on a barbecue for us. He was giving away free food that was going to spoil in his store. It was the best meal I'd ever had.

That evening we found that a spokesperson for the police department had gone home only to find that his wife and two children had drowned. He shot himself. Hearing that really affected others in the department, as many of them had no idea what had happened to their families, either.

On Wednesday night, things in the neighborhood got worse. Patients at Touro hospital began to die. Because of the depth of the flood, there was no way to evacuate them except by helicopter. That was when the 24-hour airlifts started. Patients were airlifted to the Superdome ramp, then to the I-10, and eventually to the airport triage center.

On Thursday, the policemen I'd been staying with were moved across the river. I stayed behind to help the firemen rescue people in airboats. There were simply not enough helicopters to evacuate all the people on rooftops and in the water. It was amazing to me the stories I heard of how people had gotten out of their houses. Often I heard about those who, remembering that during Hurricane Betsy people had died trapped in their attics, brought hatchets into the attic with them to cut their way to the roof.

We went out in groups of twos or threes. When we found someone in the water or on the roof, we'd pick them up, and bring them to the nearest dry interstate. Some people had spent two or three days on their rooftop. We didn't pick up those who obviously could walk out, but instead went straight out to Gentilly, the Ninth Ward, and New Orleans East. Those were the areas surrounded by water. Sometimes, when we passed those who could walk out, they shot at us. These were the ones who were shooting at the helicopters when the helicopters flew past them. They showed their displeasure at not being carried out by shooting at the rescue people.

On one occasion, I was in a large boat that held twenty or so people. We approached a house on Franklin Avenue with several people on its roof. There were a few women, some children, and two men. We got all the people off except a very large woman and a tall, thin man. He was the one who had helped get everyone off the roof. When the woman jumped into the boat her weight pushed the boat away from the house. The man, apparently fearing that we were going to leave him stranded there, jumped toward us trying to reach the boat. He missed and went under. When I looked up all I could see was a ring in the water where he'd gone down. Everyone on the boat was screaming his name. We turned the motor off and I tried to find him with the push pole. I couldn't, so I dropped it and leaned over as far as I could into the water where he'd gone down. I almost fell out of the boat myself. Reaching as far as I could stretch, I felt the top of his shoulder. I grabbed hold and yanked as hard as I could. He came up; his eyes were as big as saucers. He didn't look like he was breathing, and I thought I'd have to give him mouth-to-mouth. Then another man in the boat came over to help me pull him in. When we pulled him up, his stomach hit the side of the boat, and water gushed out of his mouth like a fountain. He gasped and started to breathe. Unfortunately, all we could do was leave him off at the nearest interstate telling those there that he was in need of medical attention. This rescue effort went on for two days. On Thursday night, I slept in my truck in wet clothes. It was eerily dark and quiet. The stars were as visible that night as they are in the country.

By Friday, the water uptown had gone down enough so that I could reach River Road, and on Saturday I felt I needed to leave and get to Jefferson Parish to see my home. At Jefferson [Avenue] and Tchoupitoulas, I saw a group of 130 to 140 people. They asked me to take them to Jefferson Parish, which I did. That was my last rescue mission. When I got to my house, I found that it had been flooded by about six inches of rain water, but was now dry. Otherwise, it and my place of business were intact.

Two events really stand out in my mind. One is the sight of the helicopters flying continuously from Tuesday afternoon until Saturday afternoon on their rescue route. They went around and around in that circle 24 hours a day. The other is of watching the Black Hawk helicopters using buckets filled with river water to put out house fires. There was this huge house on Camp Street that was burning out of control. The chopper pulled up a bucket of water from the river and dropped it on the house. The fire was snuffed out immediately. It was totally amazing; swoosh, and it was out. The next day I saw another fire put out. I was with the firefighters, and we were standing around helplessly watching this two-story house burn. There was nothing we could do about it. Suddenly the chopper flew up with its bucket full of water hanging below it. Just as it approached the house that was on fire and started to drop the bucket of water, a wind came up and blew the bucket a little to the side of the burning house. The water dropped out of it and struck the house next door. It was a single-story house, and the weight of the water buckled the roof inward, crushing it. The windows blew out, and the furniture came rushing through the windows and the doors.

September is just a blur. In October, I got seriously depressed. It was like a withdrawal of some sort. For two weeks I was involved in this intense situation, almost like being in a war. There was this huge adrenaline high, and then it was all over. I had developed such a bond, a deep kind of camaraderie, with the men I was working with. Then the bond was suddenly broken. I felt such a loss of something. Now I have this sense of separateness, of isolation, from those who didn't have this experience. It's as though others have an overview, and I don't. My view is narrow. It is only of the events I was a part of. I finally am beginning to work again. My wife still cannot understand why I didn't evacuate. I guess I'm the type of person who dashes into a burning building while everyone else is running away. One thing I did learn. I learned that heroes are not born. They are made on the spot.

We Still Didn't Have the Big Picture

Donovan Livaccari
As Told to Sylvia Schneller

Donovan Livaccari is an NOPD officer working in the Fatality Investigations Unit in the Traffic Division. While his family sought safety in Houston, Livaccari's unit was assigned to control looting.

Because I am a policeman, I'm not able to evacuate for a hurricane, but I insisted on Saturday that my wife and daughter leave. On Sunday morning, they left with my parents for Houston. The first night, however, my wife decided to stop in New Iberia to stay with her sister. On Monday, she continued on to Houston where she joined the rest of my family, two of my sisters, my parents, my grandmother, and several dogs, at a hotel in the Woodlands area. She and my daughter remained there for several days, until it was obvious that they would not be able to return to New Orleans any time soon. At that point, she moved first to be with her family in Chicago, where she is from, and from there to Florida, to be with her grandmother. I was relieved that they agreed to evacuate and found family to be with, as I was unable to spend any time with them or take care of them in any meaningful way.

The entire traffic division [50 officers] was stationed in a vacant office building on Poydras Street. We moved into the building on Sunday night. Early Monday morning, being asleep in one of the corner offices with large windows, I was awakened by my captain and told to move into the center of the building. Through the window, I could see the roof as it blew off the Pan Am Building across the street and air conditioner ducts flying by. Everything was airborne.

Around 11:30 that Monday morning, when it looked as though the worst of the storm had passed, my captain, a lieutenant, and I left the building to both check on the condition of the city and to check on our homes. My captain lived in the American Can Company apartment building, the lieutenant lived in Lakeview, and I lived in Lake Vista. Although the wind was still blowing at approximately 70 m.p.h., we had no trouble reaching my home in Lake Vista. There was no damage except for some large trees down in the neighborhood. The streets were dry. I felt relieved to find the home that I'd moved into just a month earlier intact. We next tried to reach the Lieutenant's house on West End Boulevard. When we tried to cross the Orleans Avenue Canal into Lakeview, we drove into water that was over the hubcaps on our large SUV. Realizing that we couldn't get to his home that way, and thinking that the flood water was from the rain that was still falling, we turned around and went to Harrison Avenue. We couldn't cross into Lakeview that way either because of the water. At that time, around 1 p.m., we had no idea that the levees had broken, so we turned around and went to the Captain's home in the American Can Company Building. He showered and changed, and we returned to our temporary headquarters on Poydras Street. When we got there, we were ordered to return to our main base on Moss Street.

We tried to relocate by driving out Canal Street but found that water was rising there. As it was no longer raining, we began to get suspicious that something else was happening. Sketchy information started to come in. We knew that the levees in New Orleans East had been breached because that morning, around 11:30, we heard a policeman calling for help over the police radio. He and his family were trapped in their attic in East New Orleans, with the water rising to their necks. We still did not realize that the 17th Street and London Avenue Canals had ruptured. Our communication system was down. The police radios were not working. There were no dispatchers. The state backup system, installed for just such an emergency, was ineffective. Without dispatchers to route the calls, the radio system deteriorated into endless chatter with everyone trying to speak at one time.

As we were unable to return to our main base because of the rising water, we set up headquarters at Serio's Restaurant in the 100 block of St. Charles Avenue. There was no power, but we were able to use the restaurant supplies that were going to spoil for meals. It was Monday night, and we still didn't have the big picture.

At one o'clock Tuesday morning, I received a call from a friend who was stationed in a building downtown on Poydras Street. As his building had a generator that was powering the air conditioners and phones, I went there to spend the rest of the night. Still being unaware of the severity of the levee break, I parked my car on the street in front of the building. When I awoke the next morning, my car had four feet of water in it. At that point, I realized that something was way wrong. All that day the water continued to rise. We relocated our troop to Harrah's Casino and watched as the water rose on Canal Street and Bourbon Street. It stopped just past Bourbon Street and didn't reach the casino. We stayed there for three days, until Friday. The water was highest on Wednesday.

We received orders to deal with the looting, particularly the looting that was occurring on Canal Street. We drove down the neutral ground, chasing looters, and arresting those that we could catch. We also were responsible for escorting the food, water, and gasoline supplies into the city. On Thursday, a lieutenant and I went to the Superdome to see if the National Guard that was stationed there had any clean clothes or water that they could let us have. We drove in one of the yellow backhoes that we'd used earlier to clean debris from the downtown end of Canal Street in order to make it passable for emergency vehicles.

Thousands of people were camped out on the outside ramps of the Superdome. About 100 dogs were tied up to the ticket window. The National Guard was able to keep [the people] relatively quiet during daylight hours, but apparently, after dark, people started to get anxious and panic. They then became rowdy and dangerous. We went into the Superdome, and it was packed. After speaking to the National Guard, we realized how serious the situation was. That was the first real information we had about the extent of the damage and the enormity of the flooding.

It was only after we'd made our trip to the Superdome that they started to move people into the Convention Center. As no one had ever intended for it to be used as an evacuation center, no police were stationed there, and no supplies were available for the refugees. A skeleton crew of Convention Center employees was working there, but they soon left. Without any realistic information, people began to spread rumors and believe them. One of the more frightening ones was that the flood in the city was getting deeper and deeper, and that soon the water from the lake would reach the level of that in the river and the city would disappear. Several times, I also heard the rumor that the city fathers had blown up the levees and carefully selected some people to send to the Convention Center in the hope of killing them and, thus, ridding the city of its problems with poverty and crime.

Many times I heard gunfire, and I saw a man blatantly walking down the street holding a rifle. We heard of gun shops being looted and received calls continuously for assistance. My most vivid memory of that time was the extent of the damage and the degree of chaos. The water was everywhere, and there was talk by the police of abandoning the city.

Eventually, lots of people came into the city to help. For the first several days there was nothing, and then the boats began to appear. They were lined up on Canal Street ready to go out and rescue people who had been stranded in the flood waters. Many of the boats belonged to private citizens, and I felt good seeing ordinary people helping others.

After a few days, the main contingency of police stationed themselves at Harrah's Casino. Our division moved further uptown to the Delta Steamship Offices. After about a week, my Verizon computer card came back on, and I was able to communicate with my family via the internet. It was great to have some contact with them and the outside world after being cut off for so long. I remembered the Lake Vista website and started using it to get information about my home and neighborhood. I tried several times to reach the neighborhood but couldn't because of the depth of the flood water. Finally, in a large off-the-ground truck, I was able to drive down Wisner to Robert E. Lee Boulevard. I made it to my house in Lake Vista only to find that it was flooded with three to four inches of water. That was very distressing as it was intact when I'd seen it just after the storm. While reading the website, I saw how many of my neighbors were hungry for information about their homes. I posted as much information as I could and tried to be as helpful as possible. There were rumors about looting and I alerted the National Guard that was stationed at St. Pius School to be on the lookout. I also helped arrange for a private patrol of the neighborhood and alerted the members of my traffic division to patrol the area more frequently.

The past three months are a blur. It seems like it was just September, and now it is the middle of December. My family and I are now living with my sister in Luling [Louisiana]. It is taking a long time to make my house livable. But worst of all is that the trauma is still continuing. Half of the city is still unbelievably devastated

I hope I have learned something good from this experience. I did see many people helping each other, just regular everyday people. But I also saw the worst of human nature. The looters were awful. They stole not just food and supplies to live on, but things they had no way of using, like television sets and electronic equipment. I have learned something about my own ability to persevere. It has helped me to appreciate the small everyday things.

I Just Need to Get These Old Bones Home

The Ferrara Family
As Told by Amy Ferrara-Smith

Amy Ferrara-Smith's grandfather lost not only his house of 50 years but also the grocery store the family had owned and operated for generations.

Grandpa glanced up into the mirror long enough to lift his faded gray hat over the small, glistening bald spot on the top of his head.

"It makes me feel better," he explained in a deep voice, pushing the first syllable of each word up as if he were jerking the start cord of a lawnmower. He chuckled and turned toward the door. "I don't like all that wind and rain hittin' my head."

I didn't tell Grandpa it wasn't raining outside anymore. I needed him to keep that cap on, to watch him walk to the car in his loose gray pants and thin button-down shirt, holding a lit cigarette in his right hand by his thigh. Outside our Holiday Inn motel rooms in Tallahassee, Florida, I needed my grandfather to look as he always did to me while wearing that same gray hat, whether he was painting yellow lines in the parking lot outside Ferrara Supermarket or sitting in his garage near the corner of the pool table in a chair whose seat had lost its padding. I needed him to remind me of what our home had been just 48 hours ago as CNN described a North American Venice in New Orleans, Louisiana.

It had been three years since Grandpa traveled outside of Louisiana and nearly twenty years before that to travel anywhere other than Baton Rouge for family funerals. While my grandmother had taken short trips to Gulf Coast towns with her friends, Grandpa typically stayed within a five-mile distance of his house. He appreciated the comfort of his own home, with his new John Deere riding lawnmower tucked away in his backyard shed and his small, white, un-air-conditioned truck parked in his driveway. He was content to sit in his old, worn chair positioned between the pool table and a self-made bookshelf stuffed with used paperbacks in his garage, and to take afternoon naps on one of the two twin beds in a room that was still called the "boys' back bedroom," as if his sons had never grown up and moved out. Two of his three children lived less than five minutes from his house, and the one who didn't visited from Reston, Virginia, at least three times a year. With his wife at his side, in the home they had built fifty years earlier, Grandpa had everything he needed in the city where he was born. And so at the last minute, it was with hesitation that I helped my grandparents into our car in which I would drive them away from everything familiar, evacuating from New Orleans for the first time in all of our lives.

We took my grandparents to our beach house on Santa Rosa Island near Pensacola, Florida, which my dad had recently finished repairing after the previous year's Hurricane Ivan left our family wondering if our vacation home had washed away into the Gulf. He replaced some of the latticework again on the yellow, raised Creole Cottage after Hurricane Dennis swept over the island two months before the threat of Hurricane Katrina, like an outstretched hand lightly brushing the tips of a flower so that the petals fall forward before springing back up again.

Now, for the third major threat this year, my mom, grandparents, two Labrador Retrievers and I rushed to the house, not to secure our belongings but to take refuge. As we crossed the bridge from the quaint beach town of Gulf Breeze to Santa Rosa Island, after five hours of driving in and out of evacuation traffic, I saw a man leaning against a piece of plywood as he nailed it over a restaurant window.

"Oh Lord have Mercy," Grandpa said from the back seat. "They're boardin' up here, too." He had already lived through 87 years of hurricane threats and hits, including the infamous Betsy and Camille storms, and he knew that a projected meteorological path wasn't accurate until it actually happened, even from revered New Orleans meteorologist Nash Roberts. The oncoming Hurricane Katrina could dance east from its New Orleans projection as it reached land and rip the siding and roof off our beach house for the third time in a year.

Driving down Via de Luna, it looked like Hurricane Katrina had already passed over the island. Stretches of sand littered with pieces of destroyed homes from both Hurricanes Dennis and Ivan had been pushed into mounds on the side of the street, like piles of legos waiting to be resorted and rebuilt. Grandma gasped when we passed a house with only three sides, as if we were looking into a large dollhouse with soiled furniture still in place. Trailers replaced houses on lots and the black asphalt of the street poked out from long patches of sand that had been flattened by heavy car tires.

I knew that if the oncoming storm was large enough, we could lose our water and electrical services and be stranded in a dysfunctional house if the bridge over Pensacola Bay broke in two, as it had done during Ivan. And so, after a quick lunch and numerous hurried phone conversations, we decided to evacuate for the second time that day. Mom shook her head as we talked over the kitchen counter about where we could go in a region of the country where the majority of the population was now occupying hotels.

Finally she suggested we call Grandpa's cousin, who had recently moved from St. Bernard Parish to Tallahassee, Florida, to live with her niece. While Grandma made the phone call, I lugged every loose object from the ground level of the house to the main story, as I had seen Dad do several times in the past two years when a hurricane threatened the Gulf Coast.

Each time I walked into the den with my hands full of beach toys and furniture, small beads of sweat tickled my skin as they dripped down my face. Grandpa looked helpless, sitting on the couch and watching his 23-year-old granddaughter move objects from the first level of the cottage.

I remember when I thought he was the strongest man in the world. He could twist a pickle jar open with one flick of his wrist and lift each of the five kids in my family into the bed of his pickup truck, where we played in piles of leaves that he had dumped from mounds in his front yard. But now his hands were wrinkled and sprinkled with bruise-like spots, and my grandmother looked ten years younger than he, even though a year ago, they looked the same age.

"We can go," Grandma said, pressing the red power button on her phone several times. I leaned a fishing pole against the staircase. "But we can't take the dogs."

Mom looked as if she'd just been told she couldn't take her child home from school. Those dogs were her babies, beings she could coddle as her own children continued to grow into adults. And now, with our family separated in the chaos of Katrina, she needed those dogs.

Mom's phone rang. When she hung up, she said that Dad and my younger brother, Michael, turned around to go to my oldest brother Gregory's house in Mandeville. We had expected them to meet us at the beach house after they closed our family's business, Ferrara Supermarket, but they left New Orleans too late and spent nearly three hours in a standstill line of traffic on the Twinspan Bridge over Lake Pontchartrain.

Mom and I whispered over the kitchen counter while Grandma and Grandpa sat silently on the couch, and I could tell by the child-like tone of her voice that she didn't want to make the decision. So with more confidence than I thought I had, I told Mom to accept an invitation she had received an hour earlier to go with the dogs to our neighbor's mother's house in Fairhope, Alabama. I would take my grandparents to Tallahassee. When the beach reopened after the storm, I suggested we all meet on Santa Rosa Island again, until we could return to New Orleans.

Ten minutes later we separated.

Traffic moved easily toward Tallahassee, contradicting the sound of the reporter on 870 am radio who talked breathlessly, urging residents in New Orleans to take their last chance to leave the city before Hurricane Katrina made landfall the next morning. Three hours later, we arrived in Tallahassee. I slept in a double bed surrounded by fishing poles on one side and a sweet, petite old lady in a green nightie on the other.

When I woke the next morning, I could hear the heavy wind sounding through the television, and I knew Hurricane Katrina was slamming her force against the Gulf Coast nearly four hundred miles away. I walked into the den and sat with my grandparents. We watched the reporter strain her voice against the wind and rain thrashing into her body. An hour later we all took a deep breath and said, "Well. That wasn't too bad."

The next two days were a blur, searching for a hotel room at my grandfather's insistence and miraculously finding one ten minutes from our relatives' house, then watching the news nearly 12 hours a day. I would hear my grandfather cough before and after smoking a cigarette outside our adjoining hotel rooms until he tired himself enough to sit back down in front of the television, where he watched his city wash away and said, over and over again, "Oh Lord have mercy. This is bad now. This is bad."

When the news told us of the 17th Street Canal breech, I thought of my friends, who lived in Lakeview, and of my high school, Mount Carmel Academy, on Robert E. Lee Blvd. I drove from the canal to my house in my mind, wondering if the water would stream into my neighborhood of Lake Vista, and still further to my grandparents' house in Lake Terrace. I watched as my grandfather pulled himself off his chair in the hotel room and walked quietly out the door with a cigarette in his hand as the news reporter described another breech, this one to the London Avenue Canal. I knew he was thinking of his grocery store on Elysian Fields and wondering if the water would climb up the walls and seep through the glass doors to ruin not only crackers and diapers but his history, his lifestyle, as a New Orleans grocer just a few months short of the business's 100-year anniversary. He thanked Gawd, in his heavy New Orleans accent, that his cousin had moved from St. Bernard Parish a few months before, which now, along with the Ninth Ward, was flooded by another levee breech, this one to the Industrial Canal.

The water was pouring into my city, making canals out of streets where I had driven just days before, taking advantage of something New Orleanians referred to as dry land. It poured freely on national television as if mocking the tears that were stuck behind my eyes, trying to push themselves past the hard lines of confidence I set in place for my grandparents.

"Our house is dry," Grandma kept repeating in the hotel room, and while Grandpa nodded his head, slowly, humoring his wife's denial, I searched the internet for pictures of our neighborhoods. I contacted my older sister, Elizabeth, in New York City through e-mail and consistently pressed redial on my phone, until I heard my mom's voice instead of a recording telling me that Hurricane Katrina wasn't letting my call go through.

"I'm on Santa Rosa Island already," Mom finally said over the phone. "We have power and electricity. You can bring your grandparents to the beach house tomorrow."

And so after three days in Tallahassee, we told our relatives goodbye and left on Wednesday morning for a house, though not quite home. Mom was there with our Labs, and not long after we arrived, Dad, Michael, and Gregory walked into the house with news that my youngest brother, Hunter, a junior at Southeastern Louisiana University, was safe with a friend in Baton Rouge. I saw tears in my dad's eyes as he let his father pull him close to his thin body, and I noticed Dad's hair was almost white, like Grandpa's.

Dad later told me that since they didn't know how long they would be stranded in Mandeville around impassable streets, they wrote letters.

Gregory wrote one to Nicole, his fiancée who lived in Arlington, Virginia, and Dad wrote one to my sister, Elizabeth. When the storm passed, he rode Gregory's bike down the road to the beginning of the Interstate ramp and flagged down a truck. He asked the driver to take the two letters to the nearest town with mail service, and a week later, when we were all together at the beach, Nicole called laughing that she had finally gotten her letter.

Although the letter writing was a creative endeavor in the anxiety of not knowing when the phones would work again, our communication efforts were more advanced in the vacation home. In fact, the beach house was a media center in our post-Katrina evacuation. CNN became background noise, like the humming of my bedroom fan, and when the station broadcast an aerial view of the city, we all leaned in a little closer to the television. My grandfather moved from the den to the front porch throughout the day, where Dad had set up a radio to air 870 AM. His body seemed stiff as he walked across the tile through the front doors to get within hearing distance of the radio. One afternoon, I offered him another cushion to put against the wicker chair as he sat next to me on the porch. He laughed softly before answering.

"Oh Lordy, Amy. I just need to get these old bones home." He got up and walked back inside the house, repeating, "Oh Lord have mercy" until the door closed behind him.

We spent nearly two weeks just a hundred feet from the same warm Gulf of Mexico waters that turned our city into something unrecognizable, and we reminded each other daily how lucky we were to have a second home. But even so, I whined about how much I wanted to go back home to continue with the same life Katrina had swept away, until I realized that my grandfather had been walking aimlessly around the house for days, uncomplaining. But it was obvious he wanted to go home, too.

The way he squirmed on the wicker chairs told me that he wanted his old chair in the garage, where he could smoke slowly after a hot lunch his wife had prepared. When he sat on our couch in front of the television and picked up the remote, I knew it was a struggle for him to remember which buttons were for volume control and which he should use to change the channels. At home, he just knew. After dinner one evening, he stood up from his chair as if he were about to give a speech. Then staring down at the table, he told my parents he was sorry he had to use the bathroom across from their bedroom often during the night. He hoped it wasn't keeping them up.

I cursed Katrina every day after that. She threw me out of my home and disrupted my life, but I knew I was young enough to start over. My grandfather wasn't. He had already lived through enough adversity in his life. He and his family had survived the Great Depression by running a corner grocery store that my grandfather later expanded into Ferrara Supermarket. Katrina took his business. He had survived a World War, started a family, and later built a house on his earnings from the grocery. Katrina took the house, too. He had spent his entire life in New Orleans. He used to reminisce about how he played pickup baseball games in an empty lot near the "old neighborhood," or how he followed a crowd of other young teenagers down an ally near Bourbon Street, where they knew they could get a few beers. I asked him once why he always woke up early and he confessed that it was habit. He used to drive to the French Market at 4 a.m. to pick up produce to stock in the supermarket for that day. I always imagined that he didn't mind making that trip early in the morning. The streets were quiet, I guessed, and my grandfather could drive through the city undisturbed, as if taking a deep breath to soothe his muscles with everything familiar. Katrina took his city, too.

I knew I couldn't watch my grandfather struggle quietly every day any longer. To me, he was New Orleans. And to me, he was dying. My city and my grandfather were both dying.

I took advantage of an opportunity to be a "visiting student" in Louisiana

State University's graduate program. I learned that the credits I earned during that semester would later transfer back to the University of New Orleans, where I had just started an MFA in creative writing. I moved into my friend's 400-square-foot apartment in Baton Rouge with her mom and another friend.

A few days after I moved to Baton Rouge, Gregory read on the internet that the power was back on at his house in Mandeville. The next day, he drove my grandparents, who were eager to get as close to New Orleans as they could, from Florida to Mandeville, and Mom and Dad stayed at the beach for several more days with the dogs.

It was in Mandeville that Grandpa went to the doctor, again. Before Katrina hit the Gulf Coast, Grandpa had finally agreed to see a doctor. He'd probably only been five times in his entire life. But nearing 90, he had lost about 20 pounds, so that his pants hung loosely over his already thin body, and his coughing started to sound heavy and desperate, as if there were water stuck in his lungs that he couldn't release. He followed the first doctor visit with some tests at Ochsner Hospital, but the hurricane came before he was able to find out the results.

So the day after my grandparents arrived at Gregory's house, they went to a satellite office of Ochsner Hospital in Mandeville.

That same day Gregory, Dad, and Mom got a pass to get into Orleans Parish, pretending they were contractors going in to assess the damage. I assumed Mom hid in the back seat. They rode on top of a makeshift road that was the levee bordering the 17th Street Canal and down Lakeshore Drive, toward our neighborhood of Lake Vista. The city looked like a war zone, they said, but our house was dry amid fallen trees and scattered debris. They drove further down the four-lane street bordering Lake Pontchartrain to my grandparents' house, and just as they were about to walk inside, Gregory's phone rang.

"Grandpa has lung cancer," he repeated to my parents. "And an aneurysm. He has three months to live." Devastated, they took this news with them as they pushed open the warped door to the one-story brick house and saw mud caked over the carpet, furniture and two feet of my grandmother's freshly-finished kitchen cabinets.

I guessed the car ride from my grandparents' house on Leon C. Simon Drive and then on down Lakeshore Drive toward Ferrara Supermarket was quiet, and even quieter still when they saw, from a distance, the nameplate on the grocery store seeming to float on the surface of murky flood water, which I imagined to look much like the fluid in my grandfather's lungs that was slowly drowning him too.

My grandfather took the news of each disaster that day quietly, I heard, as he did most things. And when I visited him after my first week of classes at LSU, I was happy to see him sitting at my brother's kitchen table in his faded blue pants and gray hat, smiling below a pair of black George Burns glasses. It was early in the morning, and he wanted to teach me how to fry an egg. I would've let him teach me how to tie my shoes again if he had offered.

Wearing that same gray hat, he sat with me while I ate, until Gregory called his name from the front lawn. My grandfather got up carefully from his chair and walked toward the garage. I felt his hand on my shoulder then, where it lingered for a few seconds, covering the entire bone as it pressed down on my thin frame. It sat there, feeling strong and confident against my body, until I felt less of his palm and more of his fingers, as he lifted his hand slowly from my shoulder and walked out the garage door. He would move again in a few days, this time to a rental house in Baton Rouge to live with his wife and daughter, but I knew he wasn't thinking about that. At that moment in my brother's kitchen in Mandeville, my grandfather knew he was going to New Orleans to assess the damage. At that moment, my grandfather knew he was going home.

The House Became an Island

Lora Crayon and Sabrina Avalos
As Told by Susanna Dienes

Sabrina Avalos and her daughter, Marigny, weathered Katrina with their friend, Lora Crayon. The women initially reveled in the excitement of the storm, but, as the water rose, they became aware of the scope of the disaster. They were eventually rescued by helicopter.

Lora Crayon, 34, grew up in the house where she passed Hurricane Katrina with her best friend and tenant, Sabrina Avalos, 35, and Sabrina's four-year-old daughter, Marigny. Lora and Sabrina, friends for twenty years, both grew up in Gentilly. Before the storm, they lived at 5210 and 5212 Demontluzin Street, sharing the middle wall of a shotgun double that Lora bought in February, 2004. Lora and her children, ages eleven and fourteen, occupied one side, and Sabrina and Marigny, the other. On the weekend that hurricane Katrina approached New Orleans, Lora's children were staying with her ex-husband, a New Orleans fireman. He brought the children to the Hilton, where they passed the storm safely with their stepmother and the rescue squad. Sabrina's mother, also a Gentilly resident, booked a room for Sabrina and Marigny at the Hilton hotel, even dropped off the key, but her daughter hesitated to use it.

Lora and Sabrina decided to stay on Demontluzin Street, but not in the house they shared. Instead, they drove down to the 4800 block, where Lora grew up, to the 4000-square foot, cypress-framed, stucco house that her family has owned and lived in since 1929. It sits on a hill about twelve feet above street level, and also happens to stand on Gentilly Ridge, a "B" flood zone, which means it hasn't flooded in over one hundred years. The house came well stocked for any disaster, equipped with a generator, gasoline, a medicine chest full of her sister's nursing supplies, and a solid supply of food and water. Sabrina felt that Marigny would be safe and comfortable there, especially because Lora's sister had young kids with a bedroom full of toys and children's videos. They prepared for loss of water and utilities by filling up the washing machine, bathtub, sinks, pots, pans and numerous Tupperware containers with water. Then they looked forward to the adventure of the storm.

"We love storms," explained Sabrina. "The wind and the rain. I love the roar of the wind, how it howls."

"Sunday night," Lora said, "when the wind started picking up, around 1:30, Sabrina and I ran down the street naked, streaking down the street, twirling our hands in the air. Just feeling total freedom. When the wind started getting a little worse, and we heard a couple of cracks of the tree branches, we went back to the porch, which had an overhang. We were safe there. We sat there for a while and watched."

"We had towels on," Sabrina added.

Marigny slept peacefully in a bedroom in the center of the house, as far away from the only window in the room as she could be. Sabrina and Lora stayed up watching the storm until three or four, and then woke up again to watch a few hours later. They sat in an alcove outside again in the morning.

"The wind was blowing from the north, and the alcove was on the north side," Lora said. "We just sat there for a while and watched the wind blow by. The ceiling fan on the front porch started tearing apart. We were scared a piece would hit us, so we went inside." They didn't seem to be scared of anything else, even as they saw the wind powerful enough to pull the aluminum roof off in strips. The battery-powered radio announced that the storm would pass through New Orleans by one or two in the afternoon.

By noon Monday, the wind died down and the water came. A foot of water turned into four feet by 4:30. For Sabrina, "That was unsettling, especially because the water rushed north toward the lake, and if anything, we would've thought it would've spilled over the levee at the lakefront and flowed south. So that was very bizarre." Gentilly residents know minor flood water pretty well, but neither Sabrina nor Lora remembers the streets flooding more than a foot at a time.

That night, Lora and Sabrina admired the startling night sky. "The sun set, and I have never seen so many stars in my life," Lora said. "The power was out in New Orleans and all along the Gulf Coast region. The lights were probably out one or two hundred miles north of here. To the south is just Gulf. It was the most gorgeous, incredible sky I've seen in my life. We lay out on the front landing. I lay out there a long time Monday night and just stared at the sky, just thinking, I'm so glad I stayed to witness this sky."

Sabrina left her friend for a little while to lie in bed next to her daughter, soothing her to sleep. When they finally went to bed themselves, Lora and Sabrina set their cell phone alarms to go off in intervals, so that they could keep an eye on the water in case it rose even higher. On Tuesday morning, it rose to five and a half feet and stopped. The house became an island.

They used the generator to power the refrigerator, some lights at night, and the TV and video for Marigny to watch Disney movies. They kept their cell phone batteries charged, but neither phone functioned to make calls or to send text messages. "It was hot," Lora said. "We were stressed out. We'd been in the house and on the porch. There was no air conditioning. We were on a little island. We were worried because the water wasn't going down. I knew my kids were worried about me." They heard phone calls on the radio that people made from their attics in Mid-City, the Ninth Ward, all over. They heard people begging for help, trapped with their kids and no way out, calling the radio for help because there was no 911 service.

On Monday, Lora had willingly gone out into what she and Sabrina dubbed "Lake Katrina," wading to her brother's house four blocks away. He had animals she thought to check on, and a boat she hoped to free, so she could use it. Unfortunately, she couldn't get it free by herself, and Sabrina could not leave Marigny alone to be the needed second set of hands. Neighbors passed by in boats, pirogues, surfboards, or whatever they had that would float. Lora hoped to hitch a ride back to her brother's, but on Tuesday, she started to see grease and oil in the water and did not want to risk immersing herself in it. Instead, they hung around the house, which had six feet of dry grass below it on the slope down to the water-filled street. Dark fish that looked like flounder swam by. Sabrina gave Marigny a net, and the child entertained herself by fishing.

Marigny wanted to go home, but she also wanted to play in the water. Sabrina explained that Marigny "thought we could go home, but I don't think she thought how we would go, or the repercussions of trying to get home, or what we were going home to. She was just more annoyed that she couldn't play in the water than anything else. For the most part, we had that generator on during the day. We'd keep her occupied watching TV or playing with toys, or we'd play with her." They kept washcloths in the freezer and placed them on Marigny's head at night to help her feel cool and fall asleep more easily.

The freezer did more than help Marigny sleep at night. It also may have saved the life of Mrs. Burke, an elderly woman in the house next door. Loraine and Louis Burke, both in their seventies, actually lived in New Orleans East, but their son, a fireman, insisted they leave their house the Sunday night before Katrina. He brought them to his aunt's house on Demontluzin, next door to Lora's family house. Mrs. Burke, a diabetic, did not bring enought of her insulin, her needles, or her other medications. She came to Gentilly Terrace in her night robe. Before the evacuation, she had surgery on her legs which prevented her from bending her knees, and she was confined to a wheelchair.

On Tuesday, Lora went to check on the elderly Burkes who she had known since childhood. She brought them devilled eggs. By Wednesday, Mrs. Burke ran out of needles. Sabrina pillaged Lora's sister's medicine chest and sent Lora across the short stretch of watery driveway to make the delivery.

On Wednesday, Mr. Burke asked Lora if he could buy two gallons of water. She said, "We have tons of water; don't pay me. Anyway, it's my brother-in-law's water." The proud man insisted that he planned to reimburse Lora's brother-in-law as soon as he next saw him. He did not want help, although his wife needed it badly. On Thursday, Mrs. Burke seemed sick and out of touch with reality. She had no insulin left. Her body overheated. That's when Lora went over and packed her in frozen sausage.

Lora had been staying close to home, not wanting to spend too much time in the oily water. She waded across the driveway, through water up to her waist, back and forth between her family's house and the Burkes. But Thursday, when Mrs. Burke needed rescuing, she ran down the street, as best she could, to a few other neighbors' houses. She walked along some of the terraced land, using it like a sidewalk, but in between each house, the driveway dipped down below the murky water level. She wanted to get a helicopter's attention. The neighbors waved white sheets and Sabrina stood on the balcony of their house in her bikini, also waving a sheet. They hadn't seen helicopters in their neighborhood since Monday, but their cry for help was heeded inside of 15 minutes.

The helicopter made its way toward their house just as a neighbor on a surfboard paddled by on his stomach. The winds were so strong, Sabrina ran inside from the balcony and the surfing neighbor held onto a crepe myrtle branch, trying not to get blown down the street. Lora was on the Burkes' porch. A guardsman rappelled down from the helicopter. Lora ran across the yard to talk to him. She explained the situation with Mrs. Burke's immobility. The man told her to get everyone ready and that the helicopter would come back in an hour after refueling.

A neighbor with a boat assisted with the move of Mr. and Mrs. Burke to the schoolyard of Saint James Major, a block away, where Lora had attended grammar school. A couple of other neighbors from the block helped get Mrs. Burke into and out of the boat. Then, they all left the

Burkes to wait for the helicopter. No one else from their block of about six populated homes wanted to leave Gentilly.

Lora and Sabrina had a big decision to make. They had heard reports of chaos at the Superdome and the Convention Center, and they did not want to go there. Lora asked the guardsman if that was their destination; if it was, they did not want to leave Gentilly. The guardsman insisted that the helicopter would carry them to a safe place. It took over two hours for it to return, and in that time, they decided to go along and help the Burkes. When the helicopter came back, they were ready to be airlifted from the house.

They each packed a duffle bag with some food, water and change of clothes. Sabrina packed liquid bandaids, alcohol wipes, sunscreen, a heating ointment for joint and muscle pain, children's fever medication, and a pack of antibiotics. She also packed her bikini and Marigny's raincoat. The helicopter returned to the house and a man dropped down from the sky with an anchor on another rope to lift the women and child. He sat Sabrina down first and then Lora on the other side, with their legs in a scissors pattern. Marigny sat in her mother's lap. Sabrina thought her legs would bruise, since they were underneath those of her friend and her daughter's, but the view distracted her from the awkward position as the anchor rose above New Orleans. She recalled, "We saw parts of the interstate underwater, just water everywhere. We knew from the radio that they had water downtown, uptown, Mid-City, and all different places, but to see parts of the interstate that looked like boat landings was incredible."

Once inside the helicopter, Lora explained where the Burkes were waiting. They found other people that had been stranded elsewhere in Gentilly waiting with the couple. The helicopter ride lasted about 15 to 15 minutes, and Lora and Sabrina found themselves comforting a crying family of a mother and two teenage daughters. When they reached the alleged safe place, they were not so sure it would be OK anymore. The helicopter had carried them to Causeway and I-10, where approximately 3,000 people appeared stuck. The masses loitered, waiting for direction, waiting for some authority to take charge and get them out of there.

There were Jefferson Parish police, state troopers, National Guard, maybe some military police. Nobody had a bullhorn. Nobody knew exactly what was going on. No one separated the elderly from the strong, the babies and children from the sick. Trash littered every inch of ground. People had no place to go to get away from their own refuse. Lora and Sabrina saw four Port-o-let toilets. The basic necessities of food and water came in the form of MREs and bottled water, but no one distributed garbage bags to collect the packaging and remove it from the area.

The EMTs assessed the Burkes and told Sabrina and Lora to make sure the elderly couple got on the first bus out of there.

"The interstate has bumps and guard rails and all of that; it was a maze," Lora said. They were on the westbound side and were instructed to go over to the eastbound side, right across from the Galleria, to wait for buses. "It was hot, the sun was beating down on us." After that afternoon's rain, the atmosphere turned into a sauna. Strangers helped them carry the Burkes in their wheelchairs over the obstructions to the other side.

Strangers in the crowd helped get the elderly to the waiting area for the buses. "We were all forced to stand out in the sun by gunpoint," Lora said. "They kept yelling 'Back up! Back up! Back up! Y'all line here. Y'all line there.' They moved the line three or four times…. At one point, they were pushing the crowd back. Marigny was standing in front of me, and I lifted her over my head to keep her from getting crushed, and Sabrina was screaming, 'I'm getting crushed! I'm getting crushed!'"

In between these arbitrary moments of pressure, people stood helpless. A woman from St. Bernard Parish fainted next to Lora. When she approached a state trooper to ask for help, he informed her that he wasn't there to help, he was there for security, and he couldn't do anything. During this limbo, standing with the Burkes in front of them in wheelchairs and wall-to-wall people everywhere around them, Lora got a call through to a sister who lives in Slidell and who had evacuated to Florida. She let her know that they were at Causeway and I-10. After they talked, she couldn't get through to any of her family members or back in touch with that sister. People in the crowd around her asked if they could borrow the phone, and she willingly shared it. They weren't happy to be there, but somehow they maintained their sense of adventure. According to Sabrina, "We had a sense of humor and laughed a lot. We were hot and miserable, but we do that at Jazzfest every year." The pushing of the crowd stopped. They could see three buses pull up in the distance, and they saw them drive away full of people. But that was it. When the EMTs started packing up to leave and trucks arrived with floodlights and a shipment of folding cots, they knew nothing else would happen.

Lora grabbed a box of five cots and carried it over her head about a hundred yards to set up near the floodlights. Marigny played with a six-month-old baby belonging to a large family set up nearby. She entertained herself by cooing at it and saying over and over how cute it was. Mrs. Burke finally admitted she needed to use the restroom. The cops came in and made a tent around her. Nurses from Memorial Medical Center, evacuated earlier that day, helped lift her off the cot so she could pee into what might have been a refrigerator vegetable bin.

The EMTs had pulled off a mile down the Causeway, and Lora could see their lights from where she stood, out of sight of her group in the pursuit of a cell phone signal. The police kept the refugees penned into a small area. Starting about 9:00 p.m., she started to get text messages from her sister in Florida who knew somebody that was coming across the Causeway.

"Her husband had some mutual friends that he knew were coming back to the area that had evacuated to Florida. They were crossing Causeway and

I-10, so they had messages to them to pick us up. I got messages from her, 'We have people coming to pick you up. Can you meet them at such and such place?' It was very confusing and I would get them in groups of five. I didn't know which one was first and which last. One would say, 'Can you walk to West Metairie?' which is south. Or 'Can you walk towards Causeway?' which is north.

"Finally I got a message, 'No time. One black truck. One white truck. Harahan policemen. Nick Nuccio.' And 'He's waiting on Airline side of overpass now. Can't wait. Hurry now.'"

Lora took off running. She was fifty feet away from Sabrina when she got the message. She ran up the overpass, around, around, around the loop-de-loop, screaming Nick Nuccio's name. When she found him, he said abruptly, "There's supposed to be two women and a girl." Lora said she had to run to get them, and asked if he could take the Burkes, too. He said no. She ran back for Sabrina and Marigny without arguing.

She arrived back at their cot area with muck up to her knees. While Lora had been struggling to understand the text messages, Marigny had asked her mother to go the bathroom. Sabrina said she would take her, but not until Lora came back, because she didn't want to leave the Burkes alone. Lora ran up and sputtered, "They're here! We gotta go!" That was all Sabrina needed to hear to pack up. Lora hugged Mrs. Burke goodbye and said goodbye to Mr. Burke. She asked the nurses from Memorial to look after the couple and wished them the best. Then, they ran back in the direction of Nick Nuccio.

Sabrina carried Marigny initially, but Lora, taller and stronger, grabbed the child and ran ahead. They stepped over cots, people lying on cardboard, in mud. When she had to climb a four-foot high guard rail, Lora handed Marigny to an older black man on the other side, so that she could climb over. Shortly after he handed Marigny back, she let go of a stuffed frog she had been carrying in her hand. Marigny cried for her frog, but Sabrina and

Lora kept moving. A flood light shone out of nowhere into their faces. Sabrina saw their rescuers, a group of fat Italian men that reminded her of "The Sopranos." They drove a white and a black pickup truck, and they had a police escort sent from Harahan to meet them there and ensure their safe return. Sabrina and Lora stood outside for a moment, surveying the big, fat Italian guys, inside the vehicles with assault rifles, generators and lots of water and food.

A man tapped Sabrina on the shoulder. It was the same man from the guard rail. He handed her the frog doll. Sabrina thought, "If he only knew that these guys were trigger happy and ready to shoot looters. The guy took his life in his hands over a stuffed animal for my baby. I just looked at him and thanked him. I couldn't believe what he had done. So we got into that truck, and we held hands the whole ride from Causeway and I-10 to Harahan."

I Was Covering the Story and I Was the Story

Kim Bondy
In Her Own Words

Kim Bondy is a University of New Orleans Alumna and former Executive Producer of CNN's American Morning. Bondy was part of the CNN team who received a Peabody Award in 2005 for coverage of Hurricane Katrina and its aftermath.

I have such a proud connection to this university. It's part of the legacy of my life here on Elysian Fields. I have a little house right up the road. My school years, with the exception of high school, were spent on or just off the avenue. My mother and stepfather are also graduates of the university. This campus is where they spent three days waiting to be evacuated in the days after Katrina. I also spent a lot of time on the edge of this campus in the days following Katrina. The corner of Elysian Fields and Leon C. Simon served as a makeshift boat launch for the 82nd Airborne. More than two weeks after the storm, there was still enough water on Elysian Fields that my brother and I (he's my next-door neighbor) had to be taken by boat to see what was left of our homes. We live less than a mile from here, and, while the campus was dry, the water was still up to the street sign on our block. *American Morning,* the show that I was working on at the time, wanted to cover the story. So as the executive producer, I was covering the story and WAS the story (as we say). What I didn't realize at the time was that my brother and I were the first people covered by national television news to return to our flooded homes. See, so much of the city was still flooded, residents weren't allowed into the city, but journalists were. You'll remember that the images shown around the world were of people being rescued, or stranded at the Superdome and Convention Center and then finally in shelters. What the Katrina story didn't have at that time was a connection to homes, neighborhoods, and communities. And anyone who knows anything about this town can tell you, it's all about homes, neighborhoods, and communities. So my anchor, Miles O'Brien, wanted to tell that story, and we began that rather painful journey right at the corner of Leon C Simon and Elysian Fields.

I still have vivid memories of how quiet the city was. The air was perfectly still. The trees had been stripped bare. There were no birds, only the military, their staging area just outside these doors [at UNO], young men and women working in extreme conditions. Their job was to patrol the streets of Gentilly by boat, looking for any signs of life and the gruesome task of marking the dead. When we arrived at the campus, it was late afternoon but still blistering hot. The soldiers were packing up for the day. I told them I worked at CNN, but that I lived just up the street and was hoping to see my home. Without hesitation, they offered to take us. We piled into a tiny motorized boat, right here at the corner; by the time we got to the Burger King, we were in four feet of the nastiest, most foul water I had ever seen or smelled. I barely recognized the houses and businesses as we passed. I did recognize the Shell station where I had bought a lottery ticket just weeks before.

We continued in a slow, deliberate zigzag fashion down Elysian Fields trying to avoid downed trees and power lines, when we finally arrived at the corner of Elysian Fields and Prentiss. In my neighbor's yard, there was a body tethered to a tree. Two weeks and a day after the storm, it was still there. I remember my brother unintentionally, poetically, stating "somebody is looking for that person." That was one of the saddest moments in my life.

It wasn't about the loss of my house and my car or my brother's house; in fact, almost everyone in my family had lost their homes. It was about the profound sadness that would be forever seared into the memory of the city. Families torn apart, ripped from their communities, knowing we would never be the same. It's still hard for me to look at the pictures from that day. There are times when it's hard for me to remember what it was like on Elysian Fields before Katrina.

One year ago today, I was sitting in the control room at CNN producing a story I knew even then would change my life. My parents had decided not to evacuate and were holed up in my house. It's a two-story home, and we had a generator, so they thought they would be safe. I had trouble getting through, so I kept trying, all while producing the show. I had one anchor in the studio, one in Baton Rouge, and a team of reporters spread across the Gulf Coast. All the while, I was furiously trying to reach my parents. When I finally got through, my mother said they were fine; the house seemed to be OK, but she wanted to know if the worst was over. I called down to my meteorologist Chad Myers in Atlanta. He said the eye wall was about to pass over the city, so the winds would pick up again. I asked my mother if she knew how to text message from her cell phone. She told me she did. We hung up, and I went back to producing our storm coverage. I wasn't able to reach her for several hours, but my brother, who had evacuated to Dallas with his family, had. My house had started to take in water. A short time later, there was more than eight feet. When I finally got through to my mom—thankfully, she had an Atlanta cell phone—I could hear the panic in her voice. She asked if I could send someone to rescue them. At the same time, one of my colleagues was broadcasting what he thought to be true: New Orleans had dodged a bullet. I called down to our Atlanta news desk to tell them that we needed to make some calls because the first floor of my home was completely under water, and it didn't make sense considering the rainfall amount. Something was terribly wrong. The communication system in New Orleans was in chaos. We had trouble reaching our reporters and producers in the field. We didn't know how much of the city was affected, but what I did know was that they certainly couldn't reach my parents by car if my house had more than 8 feet of water. When I reached my mother again, she was across the street at St. Raphael. She had been rescued by boat. There was a moment of levity when she rushed me off the phone because she was "helping to save people".

As the phone cut off I thought "good, she's busy." The last text message I got from her was about 9 p.m., simply saying she was OK.

For the next three days, I worked around the clock producing extended coverage of *American Morning*, trying to get help to my parents, and trying to reach friends who had stayed behind.

A key turning point in the Katrina story came by way of a personal phone call to my home from former mayor, Sidney Barthelemy. His voice was shaking. He wanted me to know we were really missing the story. He said New Orleans was in no way prepared to go this alone. We needed federal help. Where was the president? He was right. Mr. Barthelemy had evacuated to Atlanta with his family. I asked him to go to the CNN center in the morning for an interview with *American Morning*. I went back to making calls; how were we going to get my parents out of New Orleans? The next morning, Mr Barthelemy made a passionate plea to the federal government, to President Bush, to come help New Orleans. Now, I realize lots of calls were being made. There were a lot of passionate pleas, but the one thing I do know after five years at CNN is that when there's a crisis, all eyes, including the White House, are on CNN.

We, as journalists, have a responsibility to tell the story, to effect change. I had a personal stake in this one. It was hard to be on the wrong side of it. I have people ask, "How did you do it? How did you continue to work knowing your parents were missing and your home was lost?" Frankly, it was easier to work through it. I had the resources of CNN at my fingertips, and I became a resource for our networks. In the meantime, my brother had made it to the Houston Astrodome hoping my parents might be there. While he waited, CNN even put him to work. He helped book guests not only for my show but for others including *Larry King*.

Finally, late Thursday night, I was still at work helping to book Friday's show when I got a call from a number I didn't recognize. It was from a producer at NBC. My parents were with him. Turns out, my parents were finally evacuated on Thursday from the UNO grounds to the cloverleaf

[I–10/I–610 interchange] in Metairie. She said she knew if she found a TV crew, she would be OK. She'd tell them her daughter worked at CNN, and they would help her. In the madness of what was happening as people were being herded onto buses, my parents spotted a cameraman and producer. My mom asked him where he worked. He told her NBC. She said that her daughter had worked there, and he took them to a trailer where some of my NBC friends and colleagues were. They arranged a pickup with CNN; my parents were safe.

It's not lost on me that I am blessed. That my family is the exception and not the rule. No other mothers could say their daughter worked at CNN and be immediately plucked from a crowd and shuttled off to safety.

I am thankful that I got to tell our story. I struggled slightly with telling my story on air until people here in New Orleans and across the country started coming up to me and thanking me for sharing my story, our story, for helping to put a human face on it, for pointing out the injustice, for focusing on the rebuilding. That's why we are all here today. This is a historic time. We all have to claim our place in it.

We Are Lucky Our House Still Stands

Jana Salmon Mackin
In Her Own Words

Jana Mackin is a 53-year-old poet and journalist who lives in Uptown New Orleans. She is a graduate student at the University of New Orleans. She and her husband, Jim, a professor at Tulane, evacuated to Atlanta, Texas and then to Sebastopol, California before returning home.

Sunday, August 28, 2005. Leaving New Orleans at 3 a.m.

Whether Hurricane Katrina makes landfall as a Category 4 or Category 5 is trivial semantics. A killer storm is heading our way, and we, along with a New Orleans diaspora of a million and half, need to get the hell out of Dodge. Like Dust Bowl Okies, we pack the back of our Chevy S10 pickup, whose limited space determines the meaning of "irreplaceable": photo albums, important papers, a laptop, camping gear, fishing rods, Miro and Degas lithographs wrapped in blankets, and textbooks Jim planned to use for his fall course in the ethics of communication. We also pack five cats in the cab—Mickey, Bonnie and Clyde, and our hurricane cats, Ivan and Katrina—and set off west on old Highway 90 through Cajun country to Lafayette, then north up Interstate 49 to Shreveport where we'll then head north again on Highway 71 to Texarkana because no rooms are available until then.

En route, an exodus of Louisiana plates clogs the highway. We join the new dispossessed, conscripted vagabonds lucky enough to escape in cars. A Cajun hauls his barking, caged Catahoula in the back of his truck. A minivan with a "faith" bumper sticker passes. A fisherman trailers "Charity," his Jon boat, packed with his valuables. Inside, our call-and-response cats testify with meowed amens to the truth of some Sunday morning preacher praising, "He's an on-time God!" As the miles pass, we finally lose WWL, the New Orleans radio station that continued to broadcast throughout the disaster. Few rooms are to be had in Texarkana, nearly 500 miles from New Orleans. Some gouger tries to stick us for $79.95 plus $15 for cats for some flea-bag room. Screw him. We then get help from the women at the Texas Welcome Center, who find us a motel room about 20 miles south. Meanwhile, the less fortunate pour into the Superdome as a refuge of last resort.

Monday, August 29, and Tuesday, August 30. Weathering the storm in Atlanta, Texas.

Sound bites of devastation as we channel surf CNN, FOX news and the Weather Channel, tracking when and where the eye of this murderous cyclops will smash into the Gulf Coast. At first, we feel relieved that Hurricane Katrina veered a little east, clobbering Mississippi. Once again, the Big Easy lucked out, or so we thought until the levees broke and Lake Pontchartrain flooded the city with an apocalypse of flood, fire, damnation and death. We watch surreal images pile one upon the other into a logjam of catastrophic overload and horror: dogs electrocuted in live power lines; the Twin Span bridge torn apart into dominos of concrete; a light house standing alone in the foreground of a Biloxi smashed to smithereens; streaming video of toll-free Red Cross numbers; corpses floating in sewage; an NOPD police officer aiming his shotgun at a smirking looter wading in the CBD mire: "Drop it, stupid!"

Yet during this catastrophic overkill, the kitten Katrina playfully growls at Ivan, and Jim hands me a brochure about the history of Atlanta, Texas. Within the strange serendipity of how calamity lays her cards out, I learn how a Dr. Salmon helped found Atlanta, Texas, in 1872. We realize we will not be returning to New Orleans in a few days or weeks, so we decide to head west to my father in Sebastopol.

My father's name is Dr. Salmon.

Wednesday, Aug. 31—Monday, Sept. 5. Westward ho: Elk City, Oklahoma;

Albuquerque, New Mexico; Barstow, California.

Look what the cats dragged in, literally, as if I were some two-headed, circus side-show freak or one of the great unwashed, damned with the mark of Katrina on my brow. We are heading west on Interstate 40 following the path of Route 66. For a few days, we stay with Jim's brother in Albuquerque, where I feel as if I'm in a decompression chamber of numbness. For hours we camp on the couch, news junkies desperate for any snippet of news from home. After the initial shock, we now begin to hear the pundits analyzing what went wrong after the levees broke. Rush Limbaugh rants how the wacko, liberal environmentalists are playing the race card. The fundamentalists revel in God's punishment of this debauched Sodom and Gomorrah. When coiffured bimbos glossed in Maybelline and Botox chirp mindless, morning happy talk while lawless dregs rape children in the bowels of the Ernest B. Morial Convention Center, I nearly gag. But I appreciate the sardonic humor of the Greyhound bus station being converted into Central Lockup. At least these looters will get their ticket punched. My husband has yet to hear from his two daughters. One evening we watch preseason Green Bay Packers play. Jim and his family are die-hard cheeseheads from Wisconsin. Packer quarterback Brett Favre is from Kiln, Mississippi, a few miles from the heart of Katrina's devastation. What is miraculous is that Katrina spared the infamous Broke Spoke, a Kiln Packer bar and mecca for rowdy cheeseheads. Little else is spared.

For years, the Superdome will symbolize the desecrated omphalos of a drowned, devastated metropolis. Am I angry? You bet. Every scum-sucking, bottom-dwelling parasite on the political food chain should be held accountable from President Bush, posing for photo-ops five days too late, to Governor Blanco, calling for a day of prayer instead of calling for needed numbers of National Guard, and finally to Mayor Nagin for pulling a Blanche Dubois, depending on "the kindness of strangers" to evacuate those left behind instead of mobilizing a fleet of school buses.

So what is the city's fate? Will the Big Easy be rebuilt as some quaint, soulless, sanitized, Disneyfied simulacra of the Crescent City, complete with historical re-enactment of Mardi Gras, a computer-generated Emeril cooking up McDonald's etouffee, and high noon shootouts that before the flood made New Orleans America's murder capital.

Will there, as Jim asks, only remain a historic marker, "Here once stood New Orleans?"

Tuesday, September 6. Sebastopol. Dad's 86th birthday.

At the end of the day, we're still at ground zero.

Can I recreate myself out of this muck? Most mornings, I cry a little as I recite my litany of loss. Then I bondo myself together and go on with the day. When we arrive in Sebastopol, I hug my dad. He says, "I'm so glad you got out of there."

* * *

The bird's-eye-view of Hurricane Katrina's aftermath [from satellite photos on the internet] offers clues to that overriding question: What is the condition of our house? Far from the putrid stench and damage, high-resolution aerial photography objectifies New Orleans into black and white grids of devastation. My husband traces the shadows and outlines of buildings. Streets and rooftops begin to materialize into landmarks. Here's Tulane University from which Jim is on hurricane sabbatical. Here, a nearby cemetery where caskets float. Here, Memorial Hospital where Jane, a nurse, triaged the dying in a pitch-black *Walpurgisnacht* peppered with screams and gunshots. "You see the best and worst of people," she said later. Finally, Jim traces the rooftop of our house. Out front, the old white Volvo floats in the fetid flood water flowing down our street. A tree has blown down. We are lucky. Our house still stands.

While this aerial photo provides us with the necessary distance to assess damage control without sensory and emotional meltdown, it lacks the humanity of our neighborhood. Where is elderly Mr. Ed, a hand-to-mouth retiree who collected scrap metal and aluminum cans? How about Donald, the raging drunk who, between gut-rot pints and Shakespearean diatribes in the street, cared for his grandson, Marcel? What of Jerome who shadowboxed to keep in shape and on Sundays preached to an invisible congregation?

Likewise, this photo fails to detect the interior shots of those worst-case scenarios stumbling around my head. Did the toxic, fetid brew of feces and death mop the inside of our house? Does decay and mold sodomize the mementoes of Jim's and my collective lifetimes, be they a dog-eared copy of Kenneth Burke's *Grammar of Motives* or a first edition of hippie-era, Monte Rio poet Jeffrey Miller's "The First One's Free?" Are Jim's Air Force medals from when he was a Vietnam-era fighter pilot rusting in their shadowbox? Is some crack-head looter, after one-stop shopping in the sanctity of my home and scrawling fecal obscenities on my walls, now wading through the toxic swill with my Dali lithograph "Apparatus and Hand?"

To paraphrase Uncle Duke: Shoot the scumbags.

———◆———

My blood has cooled somewhat. Memories of a porcelain birthday angel, the old Underwood typewriter, a vintage Quicksilver Messenger album, and letters from my dead mom are fading in the afternoon light of the California dream of my childhood. It's nearly harvest time. The vineyards are ripe with grapes soon to be fermented into wine. For a while, I can forget how I wept in a restroom stall near the Lost Hills Travel Center after someone asked, "Are you on vacation?"

I Am So-and-So and This Is My Social Security Number

James Welch
As Told by Susanna Dienes

On August 28, 2005, James Welch evacuated to Shreveport, Louisiana , where he worked to give legal guidance and emotional support to hundreds of people stranded in shelters.

James Welch, staff attorney for New Orleans Legal Assistance (NOLAC), initiated interviews with each Katrina evacuee at the FEMA center in Shreveport with these questions: "Are you having trouble sleeping at night? Are you having headaches? Are you fighting with people for no reason? Are you crying for no reason? Do you feel depressed for no apparent reason?" During that month of September 2005, he rarely received a "no" answer. Then he would say, "Well I'm not a doctor, but I'm having some of these same problems." Welch, an evacuee himself, suffered from recurrent nightmares. "I was in a room and it was a bright, sunny day and then suddenly the room would begin filling up with water and everybody would become panicky." Welch felt chronically tired and had no appetite. He knew a lot of what the evacuees were feeling. "So I told them, first of all, you're probably having post traumatic stress disorder and at some point you're going to have to deal with that with a doctor. Now let's talk about your legal problems."

NOLAC is part of Southeast Louisiana Legal Services, which provides free legal aid for financially disadvantaged citizens facing legal problems. Welch, who has lived in New Orleans since 1976, has worked for the agency since 1985. Welch and his boyfriend, Linton, who is also a lawyer, own a house on Burgundy Street in the Faubourg Marigny. They evacuated for hurricane Katrina on the morning of Sunday, August 28th. They took their two cats in the car. Linton drove the whole way because Welch has chronic back pain. They began their journey to Shreveport, where they both grew up. It took them eight hours to drive 400 miles including stops to eat, stretch and clean up after a disgruntled cat.

In Shreveport, Welch, Linton and their cats stayed with Welch's mother and stepfather in the house in which he grew up. On the first working day after the hurricane, Welch called Legal Services of North Louisiana in Shreveport to discover that Alma Jones, the head of the local agency, had already spoken to people from NOLAC and that she had space for him in her office. She told him to come in after Labor Day. In the meantime, a neighborhood friend of theirs in New Orleans, who had not evacuated, called them in Shreveport from a working payphone in the French Quarter. He informed them that their house had no damage at all, except in the back yard; a thirty foot avocado tree had fallen over. The friend gave Welch the number of the payphone from which he was calling, and they made plans to keep in touch by calling at appointed times.

Welch looked forward to getting to work. He wanted to go out into the shelters. A large number of New Orleans residents had evacuated to Shreveport, and many of them were at the Hersch Auditorium. At the office of Legal Services of North Louisiana, he sat down with his colleagues to talk about what they should do. Welch knew what he thought they should be doing. "What we need to do is go to the shelters and talk to the people now." His colleagues balked at this aggressive tactic. Welch explains that most lawyers are an impaired species. "The problem with lawyers is that they have tunnel vision and all they can think of is, 'Is there a case in it?' or 'Where's my computer?' or 'How do I research this?'" While Welch felt that a certain amount of that line of thought was necessary, he also felt that, in the moment of crisis, all of that was "sort of unimportant."

"I kept saying, 'We've got to go to the shelters; we really need to go to the shelters. The people need help now. It doesn't matter if we don't know what to tell them. We can just write their problem down and tell them we will try and get back to them.' I felt like what they really needed was some kind of psychological help more than [anything else]." What seemed like the most practical idea in the world to Welch became an overly complicated mission for others who hesitated to throw themselves into the center of chaos. It took a couple of weeks for Welch to convince his colleagues in North Louisiana that he was right. Until then, he busied himself at the office, starting by getting a new Notary seal so that he would be able to prepare affidavits for clients and by changing his contact information in the Louisiana State Bar Association's (LSBA) website.

Within two days lawyers and reporters from around the United States began calling him at the office in Shreveport. He has no idea why his phone rang so much because he did nothing to advertise himself as a spokesman. In the office, he helped clients with simple affidavits, some of them written by hand. "Mostly they were for power-of-attorney for people, or to state, 'I am so-and-so, this is my social security number,' so that they could get their FEMA money, their Red Cross money and basic stuff like that. 'I want so-and-so to have custody of my child while I'm up here' because they were separated from family." Welch filed a lawsuit for one woman whose husband had visitation with their children, but he took them to Atlanta and refused to bring them to her in Shreveport where she was staying. She had left her documentation of the custody agreement at home when she evacuated. Welch had her sign a notarized statement and they drafted a petition saying that she needed to have her children brought back. Welch took it to the court in Shreveport. The clerk accepted the paperwork, but the judge would not sign an order that would require the father to come to Shreveport so that the mother could prove her case.

The judge, in fact, would not have signed anything because of an executive order by Governor Blanco suspending trial dates and other legal actions. "The judge interpreted that order to mean that he was to sign nothing of any sort by anybody about anything even if they were dead." Welch felt understandably frustrated, but fortunately he had the support of three of his NOLAC colleagues in the Shreveport office. They did not give up.

The NOLAC lawyers in Shreveport worked up fliers to take to the various centers where evacuees were staying or where they received services on a regular basis, to publicize the availability of free legal advice. About two weeks after Katrina, Welch carried some of the fliers over to an evacuee center at LSU Shreveport. He asked a Red Cross representative for permission to post the fliers. The representative seemed taken aback. "Where have you been? Where have you been? All of our people are gone. You're welcome to put up signs, but it's too late. You waited too long! People have been asking where to get help for their legal problems. Why haven't you done something?" The next day Welch talked to Alma Jones again about working in the field.

Welch took Andy, a volunteer and fledgling law student, to the Hersch Auditorium. When they arrived, they encountered a private attorney who had set up a table with pamphlets, forms to fill out and laminated business cards. "I came in, and I told him who I was with, and he said, 'Well, you're not with the LSBA, are you?' and I said 'No.' 'Well good,' he said, 'because Red Cross has already said they don't want anything to do with the LSBA because they've been so unhelpful!'" In addition to this attorney, a volunteer lawyer from the Shreveport Bar Association was there, and she confirmed the Red Cross's denunciation of the LSBA. Welch and his apprentice stayed for five hours and talked to several evacuees.

On the ride back to the North Louisiana Legal office, Andy told Welch that he had emailed the LSBA three times to find out if he could, as a beginning law student, volunteer in Shreveport, but he had not received a response. Welch had been willing to give the LSBA some leeway because the organization had to evacuate to Lafayette, and Welch could see how it would be challenging to keep things going. But after spending five hours at the Hersch Auditorium, this detail about the Association ignoring the request of a law student to be put to work sent him over the edge. Welch picked up the phone.

"I get a little excited," he explains, "I admit that. I got really excited. I called up the Bar Association and screamed so loud that everyone in the building heard me, and I said 'How many more people have to die before you do something to help them?'" Welch got transferred up the chain of command on that phone call, until he finally had the attention of Mr. Frank Neuner, the Association President. "I said, 'You're not doing anything to help these people. They are desperate. There's a private attorney. He's got his laminated cards in a basket, and he's running the show down there, and Red Cross told him to tell you that they don't even want you there now. They wouldn't take you if you came with a million dollars!'" Shortly after that point in the phone call, Mr. Neuner hung up on Welch.

The next day, Welch called the LSBA to apologize to the people he had yelled at along the way, to Mr. Neuner and to the president himself. This was not easy for him to do. "My problem was, here we had failure from the president of the U.S., his man in charge, who we've now found out had blatantly lied. Governor Blanco does not realize she has the authority to call out the national guard. The mayor said he didn't know what to do with all those school and RTA buses and they never opened up this shelter at the convention center. Every day we see this on TV. I'm looking at it, and actually, I saw some of my old clients at one of those centers and heard the complaints they were making. I told Mr. Neuner that I was upset that it seemed like this was just another example of the authorities not doing what they were supposed to do. And the LSBA certainly represents one of the most elite groups in the state, and you have an obligation. We take an oath! We will help in times of need, and that we will do it for free, and we're required to do all this pro bono work. And they weren't doing it!"

Welch did not return to the Hersch Audiorium. In mid-September, a FEMA center opened in a church, and Welch went there almost every day for about two weeks. He spoke to over a hundred people. He initiated each interview with the question, "Are you having trouble sleeping at night?" When he got around to talking about their legal problems, he explained that "most of the time, it was just me giving them a simple answer." If he didn't know the answer or needed to follow up with someone, he'd call the person back over the weekend from his mother's house. Although he couldn't get back to everybody, he believed it was a pretty effective way of helping people, and they often told him they felt better after speaking with him. "The main thing is, I'm in an agency that's supposed to help people. It's what I thought we needed to do. So I did this for a real long time, and then we started working out a schedule." Local lawyers began to come in, and someone set up a computer. Little by little, a system came together.

Welch, Linton and their two cats returned home on October 7th because NOLAC called and said they needed him. Welch loves New Orleans, and he cares deeply for its people. "I live in New Orleans because I want to live in New Orleans. This is the only place in the United States I feel like is home to me. Maybe it is because of my weirdo personality or because I'm gay. Because I like black people. Because I love good food." His clients told him the worst thing about being in Shreveport was that the food tasted so bad. But Welch says, "The people in Shreveport, certainly at the legal services office there, were more than kind to us and very concerned about, not just the situation, but how we were doing, and that kind of thing. I did not personally hear a lot of this talk about Sodom and Gomorrah destroyed. I heard people say that and heard that people did say, 'Now the blacks are gone!'

"To tell you the truth, I told every black person, 'Please come back. We need you. It is not New Orleans without you.'

"People ask me, what's so great about New Orleans, and I told them this in Shreveport: 'It's got the greatest soul in America.' And I think that's true. When you think about it, without the black culture, a huge part of that soul is going to have a hole in it. And that's what distresses me a great deal."

Bill You're Alive!

Bill Scheile
Interviewed by Nicole Pugh

Bill Scheile is a French Quarter fixture and a self-described amateur historian who works as a server at Muriel's restaurant. In the interest of posterity, Bill remained in the city during the hurricane and watched as his neighbors evacuated.

Tell me, what was going through your mind in the days before the storm?

The day before I was supposed to work a double. When I had left the night before, they weren't sure if they were going to serve dinner the next day, but we could do lunch. They would have to see about where the storm was and what it was doing. I walked up, and there is Eldo [a Muriel's employee] nailing plywood to the windows. "I'm guessing we're not opening for lunch," I said. "No," he said, "We're running for the hills." I go in, get my coffee and sit down with Eric, the owner. He's like, "Yeah, its coming. We're grabbing the girls and getting out of here. Do you want a ride?" "No," I said, "I think I'll hang." "Okay," he said, "I have a suite at the Place de Armes hotel, on the fifth floor. You are welcome to it."

"Do you have enough cash on you?" he said. "I got some cash," I said. "If there is anything around here you want, grab it," he said.

He took me over to the hotel and hooked me up with the room. It was a beautiful suite with huge, arched windows that maybe aren't the best idea during a hurricane. Then I went back to the restaurant and grabbed some Creole snack mix and some alcohol and candles. I dropped the stuff off. Then I came to Flanagan's [bar on Dumaine Street] of course, where we started the hurricane party. I hung out until about 1:30 or 2:00. It started raining, and I went back to the hotel and crashed.

When I woke up, the walls and ceiling were vibrating. The room had these big storm drapes behind the other drapes. They were really heavy, like some sort of vinyl stuff to keep the glass from flying in. I had those all closed down. I sat there for a while listening to all that was going on. Then I thought, "I have to see!" So I opened the drapes. It was totally *Wizard of Oz*, with balconies and trees flying past. I was watching chimneys fall. I was looking down, and I was not seeing water rising. There were swimming pools full of trees and gardens and courtyards trashed, but no water. This is good, I thought. There were a couple of points [in the night] when I had the door of my room open and the door of the stairs open. I had my backpack right next to the door in case I had to bail because the roof was doing this kind of in-and-out thing. I was thinking, "this could go any minute."

When the storm died down, it was sunrise. It was six or seven, I guess. I could see that the winds were just kind of breezy and it was drizzling. I went back to Flanagan's and everybody yelled, "Bill, you're alive!" I have been getting that a lot lately. I pretty much hung out at Flanagan's the whole next day. I think I went back to the hotel one time. The gate was open. I went looking for a concierge, so I could drop off my key, but I couldn't find anybody. Nobody was there. Then I went back to Flanagan's. There were about twenty people and beaucoup dogs and cats scattered everywhere. This was a refuge.

When the insanity began—you know, all the looting and the fires and all of that, and no public security whatsoever—there were times when I saw cars with their rear windows blown out. Andy and the boys just barricaded both ends of the street, and there was a huge pile of assorted ammunition on the bar. Everybody was armed to the teeth for about five days. They just held the block. There were several families in the hotel on this corner. They had evacuated their housekeeping staff into upper stories, and they were here as well.

Were there things happening around you during that time?

Not on this block and not much in the Quarter. There was looting, but it was more what I would call reasonable looting. People broke into grocery stores. The fact that they were taking cigarettes and booze as well as food. Well, it was *there* and it's the Quarter, so cigarettes and booze could be considered a necessity. And you just survived a hurricane, so I do think that that is in order.

It was on the fifth day that the Army got here. I remember there was a bunch of us on the balcony as they were coming down Royal Street. They used the Airborne to seal the Quarter, and they were coming down Royal to close off Esplanade. There was a fire fight right there. That was in the evening, and it lasted like three and a half hours. My advice to anyone: if you are thinking about shooting at the 82nd Airborne, don't. You are just going to piss them off. After that, we were like, "Good to see you guys! Thanks for coming!"

On the sixth day, when there were troops all over the place, there was this vehicle, kind of an armored-plate thing, not really a Hummer, a little smaller than that. This officer got out. He goes, "I know you all have been doing what you have to do. My hat's off to you. That's great. You guys are fantastic. But would you do me a favor? Don't walk around with weapons that my guys can see because it kind of makes them nervous. That little machete, that is cute. You can keep that. Just put it away."

My experience with the army the whole time—and I have heard other experiences with them in other areas that were different—was totally cool. They were just fabulous. Also, the whole crew here at Flanagan's was totally amazing. They stayed for 12 days. Then they said, "It is time to go because it is not getting better." They gathered everybody who wanted to go and made sure that everybody went some place where they knew people.

So at that point you could have gone, but you decided to stay. Why?

I'm an amateur historian. I had to watch this go down. I've never been in a city that has been this dusted with irony, plus they left me with all this food, liquor, and cigarettes.

We [those who were left] moved into a hotel here [on Dumaine Street]. They passed on the master key as the last of them left and said, "Here, it's your house now." I actually stayed there for a couple weeks, and then people started leaving big time. That was before Rita. A friend of mine over on Dauphine is the chief engineer of a hotel in the Quarter. He had evacuated his mom [to that hotel]. She is elderly and diabetic and needs special care. She wouldn't leave the city. He was there with her. We ended up gathering a few souls together, and we had a little tribal unit over there. Everybody pooled their resources. It had a swimming pool, so we hauled water to flush toilets, which was very nice. We had a five-gallon bucket that we dropped off the balcony into the pool. We would haul it out and put it on one of the housekeeping carts. After they got all the looters cleared out—it was the 82nd Airborne who did that for us—we just went through the area, a whole bunch of us, and we just cleaned. We flushed toilets and got the bugs out. People had left stuff lying all over the place.

And there was still no power?

No power.

Did you have access to any media resources? Any radio or TV?

We were hooking up car batteries to a TV. There were a lot of car batteries, and almost everybody had a radio. We would have little tribal get-togethers at coffee shops and watch TV. It was definitely a community experience. We got down to probably about 40 people left in the Quarter, those who stayed throughout.

My friend Arlain, I kept trying to get her to join us. She was like, "No, no." With her, the army would check on her once, twice, sometimes three times a day. They would say to her, "There is free transportation wherever you want to go. We're the 82nd Airborne, baby. We can get you anywhere." They brought food and water.

I was talking to this one bunch of boys from North Carolina who were with the National Guard. I said to them, "It is good living on these MREs for about three days. Some of them are pretty darn good, and they all have candy. But that little packet of toilet paper in there, what's that for? To blow your nose? Cause you don't need it for anything else." Of course they fell down laughing. "You're right, you're right," they said. "They will bind you up, but if you eat some canned fruit or a couple of spoons of jelly or jam, that should open the gates." The next day they sent me a basket of fruit.

What about Hurricane Rita?

When Nagin did his midnight speech saying that, "Within 48 hours, we are going to kick in the door and drag you out if you haven't left voluntarily," I had several army units and police departments, like New York City and San Antonio, that I had gotten friendly with, stop by. They said, "We are right here. If anybody, anybody at all, tries to kick in your door, just holler. We're not going to let that happen." The head of the services here came on immediately after Nagin gave his speech and said, "We are not a law-enforcement agency. We are not kicking in anyone's door." A lot of people *did* leave when they heard that, though. Others refused to leave because of their dogs. They were not going to leave their dog to go to some doggie concentration camp where they would probably never find them again. They were saying, "If I can take my dog, then fine, I will go." The 82nd Airborne was [allowing dogs to go]. They were like, "Sure, get in the car. Grab your stuff. Come on, all three of you, mommy, daddy and puppy." Several people left on that.

As people started coming back, how was that?

Before Rita, property owners and business owners were given a window to come back. Quite a few people, like Arie and Louise over at Mojo's, came back then and didn't leave. They just immediately started cooking and feeding people. They put tiki torches in the bar so people could see. They wouldn't take anybody's money unless they had a nametag on. There were several places that were doing that.

There was a lot of hugging. When Andy and Dan got back, they nearly caused a collision on Decatur screeching to a halt in their van, yelling, "Bill, I was sure you were dead!" So that was cool.

As an historian, how do you view this event?

It kind of changes my concept of the military. [They're] not as buttoned down as I would have expected, a lot more go-with-the-flow. Of course, we were dealing largely with National Guards, and this is their home, too. They are walking through here, and they are just going, "Dude, I'm so sorry." We were dealing with them from all over the country, New Jersey, North Carolina, Texas, Minnesota. They are out there viewing the four parishes that are gone. They were imagining if half of their city was destroyed.

I Don't Have Friends I Have Associates

Chiquita Carpenter
As Told by Dena Vassey

Chiquita Carpenter was a senior at Frederick Douglass High School in the Lower Ninth Ward when Katrina hit. She stayed in shelters for six weeks with her family until they received a FEMA trailer in Bunkie, the small town in central Louisiana to which her family evacuated.

"You joking, right?"

That was Chiquita Carpenter's typical response whenever a teacher asked her to get out her homework. With eyebrow arched, chin jutted out, and head bopping from side to side to accentuate her words, she'd continue: "Oh, no... Uh-uh... I don't got it... I am serious." After hemming and hawing for a few moments, with a glimmer in her eye and a wide smile on her lips, Chiquita would finally take out her completed work and set it neatly on her desk. She always had her homework. She also had to have the last word.

"Psych!"

Before the storm hit, Chiquita Carpenter was a senior at New Orleans' Frederick A. Douglass High. She had a decent grade-point average and had taken the required courses in order to qualify for TOPS, Louisiana's Tuition Opportunity Program for Students, which would pay her tuition to all public and some private Louisiana postsecondary institutions. The skinny, loudmouthed, red (i.e. light-skinned) young lady with the big smile was well-liked among her peers and teachers. Part African, Native American, and Creole, Chiquita lived in the Ninth Ward with her parents, three older brothers, two twin sisters, one younger brother, and a pet Shih Tzu called Precious Girl. Another older sister lived out in Michoud [Michoud Boulevard, near Six Flags in New Orleans East] with her husband and their two children. Her grandmother, another older brother, and many other extended family members also lived in New Orleans.

Before the storm, Chiquita enjoyed going to the lake [Lake Pontchartrain], Six Flags, and the movies. After school, she and her friends, Brittany, Shaneta and Amira, often took an RTA bus down St. Claude Avenue, which becomes Rampart Street. They exited at Canal Street where they would pass the time shopping. On the weekends, Chiquita would watch a movie, go to a block party, or "go by a friend's house or a family member's house." She had a good life. All of that changed when Hurricane Katrina ravaged the city her family called home.

"As soon as we heard about the hurricane, we decided to leave. As I packed my clothes—underwear, three outfits, and a pair of shoes—I was happy to leave," she said. I didn't know it was real this time. Thought it was going to be like last time [Hurricane Ivan] when we rode it out and went back home. So we just started driving. We went to Texas 'cause my auntie lives there."

Chiquita and her parents, twin sisters, and two-year-old brother left their pink, double-shotgun home and fled west as planned. When they stopped at a gas station, someone told her weary father about a shelter, so they turned north, ending up at the St. Anthony Knights of Columbus Hall in Bunkie, Louisiana. The Carpenters stayed there for two weeks.

According to Chiquita, "The K.C. Hall was very nice. Everyone enjoyed staying there, and we all became one big family.

"Then we had to move to another shelter, and it had beaucoup people. I really didn't like the Haas Auditorium."

Chiquita felt fortunate to be able to take a shower, and her family purchased air mattresses for sleeping. Others slept on cots, but there were too many people, and living conditions at the auditorium were certainly not ideal. As Chiquita put it, "We had some privacy but not enough. The food was the worst of it all. They had food that looked like pet food, so we bought a lot of fast food and junk food."

The Carpenters spent more than a month in Haas Auditorium before receiving a FEMA trailer in St. Landry Parish. During their weeks in the shelters, the Carpenters were frustrated and angered by what they learned of New Orleans. Because their cell phones were no longer functioning, they had to rely on television news for information about their hometown.

"We couldn't face that it was for real; we couldn't believe. One time I cried while watching the news [because of] how they had those people on the bridge, and I knew my family was out there," Chiquita explained. "Seeing kids hold up HELP ME signs, NO FOOD and NO WATER signs. I was anxious to go back home and worried about my people."

That was before she knew that her home had been destroyed. The Carpenters found out more personal news when Chiquita got a new cell phone in September, and her father made a trip back to New Orleans at the end of that month. According to Chiquita, the Carpenter's house had flooded "to cover the beds." The ceiling had collapsed in Chiquita's room. Everything else was ruined. And Precious Girl, the Shih Tzu they had left behind for lack of car space, could not be found. But there was even worse news to come. Her uncle, his wife, and their daughter drowned in the flooding of the Lower Ninth Ward across the canal.

At first, life in Bunkie was boring at best. Chiquita explained, "It's so borin' here. Nothing to do at all. No movies out here. I don't see how they live out here. This is miserable. They don't know what the RTA is, for real. They don't have nothing down here. Have to go to Alexandria for anything."

She went on to describe her new school, Bunkie High. "I just can't focus. I ain't used to this school. Mostly white, a few Asian and blacks. Always gone to mostly black schools before. They don't have uniforms like Douglass, but we have to keep our shirts [tucked] in. This school is wack. They don't have hallways; it's like portables. The English teacher teaches like we in college. The rest of my classes straight. No fires [waste paper basket fires were frequent at Douglass], but we had a bomb threat last week."

When asked if she had made any friends or was dating anyone, Chiquita was quick to respond, "I don't want no Bunkie boy!" She continued, "I have associates here, not friends. I'm leaving next September going to Texas or Atlanta. I don't know how long [my parents] staying. I'm gonna go to college, but I don't know where 'cause I don't know where I'm gonna stay at."

Chiquita eventually adjusted to life in Bunkie, though she would have preferred to have been somewhere else. She went to the senior prom, and she found a few associates. She graduated from Bunkie High in May 2006. She is still intent on getting out of Bunkie, but she won't be returning to New Orleans.

"No Indeed. New Orleans ain't gonna never be the same. That's why I ain't going back, but I will be visiting a lot. The house is destroyed. My parents was talking about moving anyway, but they didn't wanna move like that. They were going to move to Mississippi. My parents still talking about moving to Mississippi, but I don't know when. I miss my family, my friends, my house and my school."

Chiquita's family, all former New Orleanians, are now scattered across several states. She, her parents, and her little brother are in Louisiana. Her older sister, brother-in-law, and their children are in Georgia. Her grandparents are in Mississippi, and one older brother is in Minnesota. Her other older brothers and twin sisters are in Texas.

When asked her thoughts about the hurricane, Chiquita's original response was, "There's nothing I want to say that you can write in your paper. I wonder why they wasn't helping people [who had stayed in New Orleans]; they was just getting in the way. As every day passed, the problem just got worse and worse. They waited so long elderly people and children could no longer hold themselves up. They began to faint. They family cried and kissed them goodbye and tried to be strong for the others. The people in jail have a lawsuit because they left them in there with no food, no water, and no lights for two days. Some people were stuck in they houses with nowhere to go and the water went over they houses and drowned them out. It seemed as if no one cared for the people still [in New Orleans]. Bush just sat in the White House like nothing just happened, and Bush, Blanco, and Nagin was playing around, pointing fingers at each other, from what I found. I don't care what no one says. I think they should all resign because that shouldn't have went down. FEMA now deserves another name: Failed to Evacuate Many Americans or Fix Everything, My Ass."

When You're On My Bus You're My Family

Oscar Cade, Sr.
As Told to Mary Sparacello

Oscar Cade, Sr. is an elected member of the Jefferson Parish Democratic Executive Committee. He evacuated with his family to Texas but returned almost immediately and used a school bus to rescue stranded victims from the crowded Convention Center.

I was here when [Hurricane] Betsy came through. My dad and brother, we stayed in the house by Hanson City [the oldest part of Kenner]. Our neighbors had a big brick house. We had to run to get to their house. We could see our house lifting up and going back down, lifting up going back down. Ships were crashing into the levee. Railroad cars were traveling by themselves. It was cold, dark, dreary; there were no lights for the longest. I always promised myself when another one comes around, I'll leave. I'll never put my family through that.

[So for Hurricane Katrina] we left and went to Dallas. I got relatives in Dallas. Hotels and everything be full. I had my son there, and they was in a hotel, but being an elected official, I had to get back and see what I could do. I left Dallas and went to McComb, Mississippi to check on one of my grandsons. Then I went to Prairieville to check on my other grandson. On the radio, I heard Governor Blanco calling all the bus drivers in Jefferson Parish to help get people out of New Orleans. My bus, I had parked it over on Bainbridge [a street in Kenner near his home]. It got water and someone broke in and got the CB, but it was full of diesel, and I just wanted to do something to help out. I went to 51 and the Interstate. Then I went to the Convention Center and started getting people to bring them to 51. It was sad; they still had standing water. There was water on Poydras [Street, in front of the Superdome]. No lights were working. It was just a sad deal. The people, their body odors were just terrible because they hadn't bathed in days.

The people on my bus, I managed to tell them jokes to get them to laugh to get rid of their sorrow. Everybody's looking over at our bus and wondering what was so funny. For a moment, I had everyone on my bus in laughter, not in tears. I told them how to stretch their money: if you have $10, you change it for a five, four ones and four quarters. An elderly white gentleman came up to me after the ride when he was getting off the bus and tried to give me four quarters. He misinterpreted my joke; he didn't understand. He didn't have anything but the clothes on his back. I gave him ten bucks; that's all I had in my pocket. It showed me he didn't have anything, but he was willing to give me what he had for getting him on this bus and getting him out of there.

I told them they was all on my bus; they were my family. I told them to look out for each other. They asked me, "Where are they taking us? Where are we going?" I told them any place would be better than New Orleans right now. I felt bad about how they put them on the bus. I guess they had to get them out of there. They were separating people who should have stayed together. That's how some people ended up in Dallas and family members elsewhere. They didn't really have it organized, in my opinion. They was taking some to Houston, some to Dallas. I took them to LaPlace for the long-distance buses. They asked if I wanted to take my bus to Houston, but I didn't want to take it that far.

I had one young man on the bus; he was so full of anger talking about Nagin, that I had to straighten him out. It took so long for help to get to these people. In Florida, help is immediate. In the tsunami, they were there in 24 hours. I hate to think about racial overtones. It almost made me ashamed to be an American. It should have been a faster response. I point the finger at local people. They should have started getting people out immediately. They'll never know the exact body count. The ocean washed the bodies out.

It Was Going to Be a Tiny Little Storm

Rebekah Reuben-Stroup
As Told to Amy Judith Reuben Pickholtz

Rebekah Reuben-Stroup is a middle-school student who lived in Uptown New Orleans and evacuated to a hotel in Gonzales, Louisiana, where she eventually attended school.

One of the weird things about before we left, which was Saturday before the storm, is that I remember watching TV the days before and seeing a little square on the bottom of the screen that said 'Hurr. Katrina' and I thought it was going to be nothing. In school, in Social Studies class, our teacher was making jokes about it, too. I thought it was going to be a tiny, little storm; I didn't think it was going to be anything.

I went to a hotel in Gonzales with my mom and with her fiancé, Jim. We were really lucky to be able to go there because he had some connection with the hotel. At first I thought staying in a hotel was cool because I never had a temporary home with an elevator in it, and I wanted to stay at a hotel, but eventually it started getting messy and trashy, and I started not to like it anymore. We spent six weeks there. The room was a little room with a TV, a microwave, and two double beds. I had my own bed. It was messy because the maids didn't come a lot.

A lot of times we went out to eat or we went to the grocery store to get food for the tiny fridge. We didn't have a stove to cook, so we ate microwave food like TV dinners or sandwiches. After a while it got annoying. I was getting sick of eating out because there were so many people in line waiting to eat or places weren't even open. We'd go driving around for hours looking for food. A lot of times the elevator broke. It was hard because we had to go up and down the stairs, and we were on the third floor. Also, there was a breakfast room for continental breakfast in the morning. It wasn't very good.

The pool was outside, but I couldn't swim in it because there was mold in the pool. It was really gross! Another thing that was annoying was there was no privacy in the room. We spent six weeks in the hotel. I didn't like not having a home.

While I was there, I went to a little school that was close by. I really didn't like that school. I thought the kids were dull and boring. The schoolwork was too easy, too. I had to wear a uniform. At the school, when people knew that I was from New Orleans, the kids got really quiet and stopped talking and looked at me. I told them it was OK, and they started talking a little more. It seemed like there was a barrier when I told the kids I was from New Orleans. Some of the kids said "sorry" to me.

I had five cats that lived at two houses, but they were left in New Orleans. When we came back, we found two cats at my mom's house. We took one of the cats to Jim's kid's house, and left the other one until we found a house to live in. Abbey, the cat we took, ended up dying of bacteria in her body a couple of weeks after she was rescued. Snowball, the other cat, lives with us like she did before, outside. The three cats at my Dad's house, Minerva, Chrissy, and Andy, were never found. We think they either died or they got rescued and are living with someone else now. I really miss my cats. I kind of hoped that the three cats all made it safely to someone else's house. I feel really sad about Abbey because we rescued her as a little kitten, and she was living with us ever since. Now, we have two other cats at our new house, besides having Snowball. They are getting used to us. Circe, my dog, is living with my dad and step-mom in Virginia. I haven't seen her in a while, but at least I know she's OK.

The first person who got in touch with us was one of my friends, Mary, who's now living in Austin, Texas. She evacuated to Corpus Christi, and then she had to leave to go to Austin because of Hurricane Rita. For Hurricane Ivan, she stayed at home in a two-story house with her family, so I was worried about them in Katrina. I asked her about our other friends, and she told me Maya was in Austin, and Paulina was in South Carolina. Later, Marga emailed me and told me she was in Florida. I really miss my friends, and I wish they would all come to where I am, but I know that's not going to happen. I'm trying to make new friends, but it's hard because they're not like my New Orleans friends. A couple of weeks ago, I found myself watching an old video from school that all of us were in, and I found myself almost crying because I miss them.

My mom told me we weren't returning to live in New Orleans because I don't have a school to go to, my mom doesn't have a job anymore, and even though our house wasn't flooded and we have our things, my mom couldn't go back because she was pregnant with my brother, Shane. She needed to go to a doctor and have a hospital to give birth to Shane. When we went back to my house to pack our things, it didn't seem like home anymore, anyhow. It was a house with my things in it. I do miss my house because of the way it made me feel, and our new house doesn't make me feel the same way. I miss my life. I loved my life in New Orleans. I had a neighborhood, friends, a school I liked, a job with Audubon Gymnastics every Monday, and my Martial Arts classes three times a week. I knew where a lot of places in New Orleans were, and I was taking the streetcar on St. Charles Avenue by myself from Uptown to where my mom worked in the CBD.

The worst thing about the hurricane is that my dad and step-mom left to go to Virginia, and they're not coming back to live in Louisiana. Their house was destroyed, and everything they owned is gone, including everything I had in my room at their house. I will be visiting them in Virginia, but it's not the same. I used to be with my dad every week for at least two days, and sometimes on the weekend we'd do something. This is the worst thing that has happened to me, losing my dad. I feel like he abandoned me.

We Have Got to Go

The Belton Family
As Told by Dena Vassey

Delton and Kenyatta Belton were both born and raised in the New Orleans area, Kenyatta in the Ninth Ward and Delton in Algiers. Fearing the worst, they packed their two children and their reluctant relatives into a crowded car and drove east.

Kenyatta Belton spent years walking the French Quarter during celebrations such as Halloween, the Bayou Classic, and Mardi Gras. Kenyatta grew up in the lower Ninth Ward at Dauphine and Caffin Streets. This was her heritage, her people. She attended Thomas Alva Edison Elementary School, St. Maurice Parochial School, McDonogh 35 Senior High School, and earned a degree from the University of New Orleans in sociology. Her husband, Delton, is a lifelong Algiers resident and alumnus of Ben Franklin High School and the University of New Orleans. They and their children, Debrian and Devin, lived in Gentilly.

Both parents were employed by the state of Louisiana. Mrs. Belton enjoyed her work at the Office of Family Support, and Mr. Belton finally had a job he loved. He was able to do things he had never been able to do before, like exercising in the mornings, going to evening church activities, and attending his children's sporting events. In September, 2005, Devin would return to Hynes Elementary for fifth grade, and Debrian would begin ninth grade. She was "super excited" to be attending McDonogh 35, a magnet school and her mother's alma mater. Debrian would also be spending half of her instructional time at the New Orleans School for Math and Science on Delgado Community College's Campus.

"I had never seen anyone so excited about starting high school," Mrs. Belton said, "and that enthusiasm excited me. I became aware of my little girl preparing herself to enter society. She wanted to be equipped for success."

The Beltons had taken their children shopping for school supplies and new uniforms. Debrian and Devin had completed their required summer reading and were ready for the new school year. According to Debrian, "If you were to tell me that my life was going to be changed like it was on August 29, 2005, when Hurricane Katrina came to New Orleans, I would have said you were out of your mind."

Since last August, Delton has replayed the events leading up to Hurricane Katrina over and over in his mind.

"Saturday morning, I remember noticing the lines getting longer at the gas stations on Chef Highway," he said. Later that day, while attending a funeral at his church, one of the speakers excused himself early because he needed to get back to work in preparation for the storm. At that time, Mr. Belton thought to himself, "I'd better gas up later this evening." He did.

Mr. Belton remembers standing in the aisle at Home Depot in Chalmette late Saturday night. He was debating whether to purchase the generator, gas can, electrical cord, and axe he had placed in his cart. "Foolishly, I made the purchase," he later admitted. He and his wife had decided to stay and "ride this one out." They were both tired of the usual routine: pack, leave, come back and unpack.

Mrs. Belton explained, "Do we leave or do we stay? It is the question every New Orleanian asked as the newest forecast of tragedy was made. Usually, my immediate family always left. We packed our bags with three days of clothes, and we hit the road. This year, however, we entertained the idea of staying home."

"I don't even remember thinking about the hurricane," Debrian interjected, "until my parents began to discuss leaving or not. It was at this point where I began to feel extremely overwhelmed inside, and that only happens when I feel like something bad is going to happen."

There were several reasons the Beltons considered staying in their Gentilly home. When they evacuated for Hurricane Ivan in 2004, their "evacuation vehicle" was totaled when another driver lost consciousness and hit four cars. They still managed to evacuate that year, but the family of four was cramped into a Ford Mustang. Lack of space forced them to leave their pet, Birdie, behind with a neighbor who never evacuates. Fortunately, Ivan did not hit New Orleans. "We were shown God's mercy once again," Mrs. Belton said. Another factor was that, up to this point, the 2005 hurricane season had only mildly affected the Gulf. Hurricanes Cindy and Dennis had pulled up some trees and caused wind damage, but nothing more. The Belton's were not only tired of evacuating; they were also distracted by personal loss. They'd held a funeral for the mother of their church on August 20th. Two days later, they lost another beloved church member.

"Our focus was clouded as we prepared to bury another member of our Christian family that Saturday," Mrs. Belton explained. "I can remember the storm being mentioned, and the last I recall about it is that it was on the right side of Florida. I don't know when it crossed over that state into the Gulf. Even with all the news coverage, we hadn't made any preparations for a hotel or anything, so we went out that night and bought a generator and an axe. I guess we were thinking a generator because we always lost power, and an axe, well, just in case."

The axe was just in case their house flooded. During rapid flooding, people can become trapped by the water and will often move as high as possible within their homes to stay dry. These unlucky people may reach the attic and become trapped there by rising water. With no window or other exit, using an axe to break through the roof may be the only way to escape. Many people, especially in the lower Ninth Ward, died in their attics during Hurricane Katrina.

When Mr. Belton turned on the Weather Channel Sunday morning, the Doppler map showed Hurricane Katrina covering the Gulf and heading straight for New Orleans. He woke his wife, who took one look at the screen before she looked her husband in the eye and said, "Do you think we might have to use that axe?" When he responded in the affirmative, she jumped out of bed, and said, "We have got to go."

"However, our leaving wasn't that simple," Mr. Belton explained. "First, we had to convince her side of the family, and my side of the family, that this was not the one to stay and ride out."

Mrs. Belton elaborated, "As I began calling loved ones, many of them had to be talked into leaving. Most of my relatives wanted to stay. The near misses like Hurricane Ivan caused a lot of people—especially those without disposable income—to stay, even when evacuating was the smart thing to do."

Among those were Kenyatta's mother and grandmother who cared for her nephew and had no means of transportation. To further complicate matters, her grandmother had just completed radiation treatment and was still very weak. She refused to evacuate with the Beltons, fearing the drive would be too much for her weak system. The Beltons refused to leave her behind. They were at a stalemate.

"It was almost as if God was reading my thoughts," Mrs. Belton said, "because at that moment the mayor came on and announced that persons with serious medical conditions could be evacuated if they were brought to the Superdome."

Even though her relatives were unwilling to leave, her husband went down to the Ninth Ward and packed them up. Mr. Belton's SUV was so packed with people and belongings that he had to strap his wife's grandmother's wheelchair to the roof and hold it with one hand. Even so, he took Kenyatta's mother, grandmother, and nephew to the Superdome, where they were evacuated to Baton Rouge by ambulance. He probably saved their lives.

"I remember driving up St. Claude Avenue with the three of them," Mr.

Belton said. "I recall the number of people going about their normal routines. Little kids were playing outside. Teenage boys were riding bicycles. Men and women sitting on front stoops watching us roll by. They all seemed to be looking at me, saying, 'Where is he going?' No one seemed to care that there was a category five storm heading our way. "I think about those people today, and I wonder if they made it out of there."

While her husband was gone, Mrs. Belton, Debrian and Devin, packed their belongings and secured the house. Even though she fully expected to return home within three to four days, there were certain things that Kenyatta Belton would almost never leave behind: an expandable file with birth certificates, shot records, social security cards, insurance identification, and a special suitcase full of family photographs. This year brought different space concerns.

"Birdie was with my godchild, but Devin had six guinea pigs that we had to take, so there was no space for my extra suitcase," Mrs. Belton explained. "Besides, we would be right back and everything would be fine, right? So I left all my precious mementos. My photos, my children's baby books that I began writing in before they were born, birthday videos and baby shoes were all left at our home. I fully expected they would be there waiting for me just as I left them.

The Beltons were on the road for 22 hours. They caravanned with three other cars, all heading east. They were hoping to avoid the worst of the traffic by heading in the opposite direction of most evacuees. Unfortunately, many of the back roads they could have taken were beginning to take on water and had closed, so this change of direction did not make travel any easier. When Highway 11 closed, they met up with the rest of their party and continued driving east on Interstate 10 until they were past Pensacola and out of the danger zone. They began to look for hotel rooms, but none were to be found west of Jacksonville.

"Due to the circumstances, the last place I wanted to be was anywhere near that much water," Mrs. Belton explained, "so we continued to search. When speaking to a hotel.com operator, I was asked about taking a room in Tifton, Georgia. I had never heard of the place, but she gave me directions, and it was inland, so off we went."

The Beltons arrived in Tifton Monday morning around ten. Mrs. Belton called a neighbor in Gentilly to let him know that they had made it, and to check on the situation there. He told her there was some wind damage, but once again they had made it through and "dodged the proverbial bullet." He spoke too soon.

Their neighborhood was near both of the London Canal breaches. As the water flooded into his house later that Monday, their neighbor was forced to climb into his attic, eventually cutting himself out through the roof. He remained atop his roof for two and a half days before being rescued. When the Beltons spoke to him again, nearly three weeks later, he described how fast the water came in and how glad he was that they had left with the kids. Having seen images of their neighborhood on CNN in their hotel room, the Beltons were relieved to find out that he was alive.

"I remember when I first found out about the water coming into the city, and how bad it scared me," Debrian said. "The first thing I thought of was my friends."

As they watched the news footage of New Orleans, they couldn't believe what they were seeing. They also couldn't accept what it meant. Though this new life seemed unreal, they knew that they had to move forward, so the Beltons enrolled their children in school after Labor Day. This step spurred a new series of emotions for their family.

"It was both a first step and a final step," Mrs. Belton explained. "A first step in trying to maintain consistency and beginning again whether we wanted to or not. This was a final step for us all regarding life as we knew it."

Starting school in this new place ended the "vacation" that usually happened during an evacuation. Suddenly, the Beltons, and especially their children, were faced with beginning a life in a new place.

"It was really hard to be in a new place in general," Debrian agreed, "but it got even harder when I started school because I felt like I was being forced to throw my old life away and start over completely. I wasn't ready for that, and I'm still not."

The transition seemed to be harder on Debrian than it was on her younger brother. According to Devin, "My sister goes to Northeast High School, and I go to Wilson Elementary. We both like our schools and are doing good. A lot of people have helped us here."

After six weeks in the Ramada Inn, the Beltons began looking for a home. "People all over Tifton have helped us search," Devin explained, "and we finally found one. It's a nice house, too. We all like it a lot."

While they settled into life in Tifton, their extended family members, who had caravanned to Tifton with them, moved away. Some went to Texas, and others, whose homes had not flooded, went back to New Orleans. Mrs. Belton found a job that utilizes her skills as a case manager at the Department of Family and Children Services. Mr. Belton started taking classes to begin another career, which he finds frustrating, especially because he had such a perfect job in New Orleans.

"As of now, I am out looking for work again," he explained. "Filling out stupid job applications and waiting for someone to judge me from a piece of paper."

The Beltons were able to return to New Orleans in the fall. What they saw there will haunt them forever.

"It was mid-October when we returned to the drained city," Debrian said. "It was the most unforgettable sight and smell ever. I'm used to seeing the city in lights all the time at night, but the night we came into the city it was pitch black, and that was shocking."

"What we saw still shakes me to think about it," agreed Mrs. Belton. "Everything was dead. The hedges I painstakingly trimmed trying to make them exact replicas in shape and size—dead. The flowerbed I loved—dead. The lawn I griped about cutting—dead. Mold covered everything I owned. And the smell! I will never forget that smell."

"After seeing what I saw, all I could do was wonder if my life would ever be the same," Debrian continued, "and think how badly I wanted my life to go back to the way it was."

"I have a problem accepting that this is now my life," Mrs. Belton admitted. "I am living in a different state. I find myself, at least once a week, commenting to myself that I cannot believe this, with the hope that it will get easier. My heart aches for all that was taken from me. I cry almost every day, but I know that this is part of the grieving process. I don't long for the sofa I used to lounge on, but for the actual ability to drive up to my home that I chose in my city where I grew up. I want to go to the homes of all those I hold dear just like I used to, but now they're all ten hours away."

"I think about the people a lot," Mr. Belton said. "I don't care about houses and buildings. I worry about the people of New Orleans. I wonder about my coworkers and acquaintances whom I never got to say goodbye to. Are they OK? Are their families OK? How are they making it?"

"I was fortunate to hear from my friends," Debrian said. "All of them made it out OK. But New Orleans was my life, the only thing I really knew. The Big Easy was, is, and will always be the greatest place ever no matter what has happened." Debrian continued, "Since the storm, and since I got back from New Orleans, I live my life day to day. It's going to be hard, but I'll make it because what doesn't kill you will only make you stronger."

"I see how this disaster is affecting my family," Mr. Belton said, expressing his concern. "Physically, we are fine. However, we are all still dealing with the mental effect of this tragedy. Often, I pray to God to give me the strength I need so that I can be strong for them. I wish that I could take away the feelings of loss that they have all expressed."

Even Devin gets sad sometimes when he thinks about New Orleans. "I kinda miss my old school Hynes sometimes," he admits. "It was really fun there. I also miss my old friends, but I also like the new friends I've made. It will be OK."

Mrs. Belton agrees. "We have been embraced and aided by a town that lives up to its slogan, 'the friendly city,'" she explains. "The kids are both benefiting from excellent, well-funded, enough-books-to-go-around schools. I don't know what the future holds where New Orleans is concerned, but I can only deal with it as it comes."

The Beltons are renting a home until the end of the school year, when they plan to reevaluate their future. For Debrian, there is only one option.

"I believe that home is where the heart is, and New Orleans was, is, and will always be my home, because my heart will be in New Orleans no matter what."

"Do we leave or do we stay?" That is the question the Beltons will again be facing at the end of this school year. According to Mrs. Belton, "At least this time the decision will not be made as a category five storm approaches."

I'm the Leak Expert

Wayne Wilson
Interviewed by Jana Mackin

Wayne Wilson has worked for the Entergy Gas Department for over 30 years. Working constantly while most were still evacuated, Wayne also took photos to document the wreckage.

You work for Entergy. What do you do?

I'm a leak surveyor. I find leaks. That's all I do. I'm the leak expert that goes around finding gas leaks in the streets, the meters, the lines going to meters. That's what I did all over the last couple of weeks. I work in New Orleans East.

I stayed for [Hurricane Betsy]. I was 15 years old back then in '65, and I don't remember it being nothing like Katrina was. I mean, we had a little bit more rain than wind during Betsy, but this was a lot more. I was raised in Mid-City. I live now in Old Metairie. I had about two foot of water, but it went down after the storm. It didn't stay. It came up and went right down, but the wind was real bad. I got a frame house off the ground and two or three times, I didn't think that house was [going to survive]. It was moving and then a few times I heard the roof and I told my wife, "We're going to lose the roof. The roof's going to go." Didn't, thank God.

Do you have family?

I've got three children and three grandchildren. They're all on their own. One lives in Kentucky, one in Texas, and my son lives here but doesn't stay with me. He was in Mississippi for the hurricane.

Entergy [said], "Do what you need to do. Your family comes first." And to get in touch with them after the storm. That's our normal procedure after the storm, and we have to make our contacts and let them know we all right, what we're going to do, what the game plan is.

But I stayed. I just thought it wasn't going to be that bad. Yeah, I was home. By that time the water was cut off, no electricity. The only thing that was working was my house phone. I was listening to the radio, and they said the levees were breaking. That's when I said, well it's time to go. It's time to pick up. Because I had no idea how bad the levees broke or how big of a break or how much water was coming. I told my wife there's no use of our staying. Nothing's going to be open, no stores. Where you buy food? No gas. I mean there's no nothing. And they didn't know how long it's going to be before everything's restored, and so when the levees broke, I said, "It's time to go."

I ended up going to Baton Rouge. I have family in Baton Rouge. And it just happened that all the gas employees would report to Baton Rouge, so it worked out for me. All the other employees were in campers. They put them in campers, and we commuted every day on big buses. They brought us to New Orleans, and in the evenings, they'd bring us back to Baton Rouge. This went on for maybe a month, month and a half.

They tried to gather all of us in Baton Rouge and find out what we were going to do when we came back to New Orleans. They hadn't a lot of preparation on the game plan on where we going to start at or where can we start at. With a lot of the areas, the water was still high. Our office on Tulane Avenue was under four, five foot of water. We lost all our trucks and our yard over there. It never flooded there before. We didn't know. Where do you start? We met every day at the Pontchartrain Center in Kenner. We had a staging area out there in the parking lot, and then we just started assessing the areas to see how much damage, which areas were safe to go in. Lakeview was still under water; New Orleans East was still under water; Ninth Ward was still under water. So where was safe, where you could drive through? We started assessing the areas, and from Pontchartrain Center we moved to Lakeside Shopping Center and from Lakeside Shopping Center we moved to Audubon Zoo. Just recently we were able to go back to Tulane [Avenue] but not to our building. Our building is still sealed up. We have trailers in our parking lot where we can report back to where we normally work at. We just don't go in the building. We just report to trailers and stuff.

[When I first came back after the storm] my wife stayed in Baton Rouge about a month and half, maybe longer, 'cause there was no electricity in my house. I'd check my house just to see if the electricity would come back on. And it was a while, I'd say a month, before my electricity came back on. But we still didn't have water, no good water, not drinking water. They were suggesting not even bathing in it at one point. So I left my wife up there in Baton Rouge. I was commuting. I was commuting back and forth every day.

They say the older you get the wiser you get, but I think it's the [more] scared you get. You might be smarter, but you fear more as you get older. Like I said, to me it was pretty bad. I won't go through it again. I'll leave the next time. I won't stay.

There really wasn't nobody around. It was like a ghost town. [Near the CBD, Convention Center] it was pretty wild. I didn't get into the Superdome, but we was able to pass by it. We had a lot of buildings we had to check and make sure the gas was off and everything was safe before we could restore everything. We had to turn everything off because we had no idea what type of damage was done or anything.

I saw a few dead bodies, not by the Convention Center. I saw one outside the French Quarter by the flood wall. That's our first one I seen. I didn't take pictures. Some of the guys took pictures, but it was kind of disrespectful, so I said, no, I don't want no pictures of any dead bodies. It was a man, couldn't tell how old he was. I think he had been there for a while. I was right off Elysian Fields and the river. Yeah, yeah, yeah, yeah. I saw a few of them, but like I said, I didn't want to take pictures of them. It was something you didn't think you'd ever see down here in New Orleans.

Like it could never happen down here.

Have you changed?

Naw. I guess maybe more people be more aware now with the surroundings like the levees and, you know, I don't know if I retire if I want to stay here. The levees and the safety factor. 'Cause it could happen next year. I mean we missed forty years. We didn't get a big one, but we could get another one next year. And I feel sorry for the ones who are trying to rebuild their houses especially like in New Orleans East and Lakeview. They've lost everything. If you rebuild like next year, you may be going through the same thing again.

I worked with men that lived in St. Bernard; some of them lived close to Violet. Some of them had 14 feet of water. I mean, I take my hat off. I work with these guys every day from six in the morning to whatever time we get off at night, and these guys have no home to go to. They don't have nothing. Everything they owned was gone, but they still out here. They out here every day. And like I said, I take my hat off to them. I had minimum damage compared. These guys are working, don't have nothing. Some of them have families that are still like in Georgia. One guy's wife in Colorado. Some of these guys haven't seen their family since the storm. Like I said, pretty strong guys to do it every day, to put the hours in, and not have nowhere to go after. They lost their vehicles. They lost all their personal stuff they accumulated over fifty years or so, their home. But they're holding pretty good.

I think we've done pretty good as far as getting the people [power and gas] back on, as far as the forecast in the beginning. They thought it would be months, and months, and months, and months, and we think we beat it so far. We've done real good with it as far as restoring the people we can restore with the time period we're doing it in.

I think personally [it will be] years and years before it will be back to anything close to what it was. I think a lot of people that lost everything, especially businesses, might not want to invest their money back down here again. They want to go somewhere where it's going to be safe.

[My wife is] doing all right. She's a strong lady to put up with me the hours I put in and not seeing me all the time, the last three months or whatever. She's a pretty good support. We don't know yet [about Christmas]. We may get Saturday and Sunday off. My wife put the tree up today. I said, "You went in the attic?" She said, "Yeah." Of course, she always put it up right after Thanksgiving. I said, "You might be sitting by that tree by yourself come around Christmas 'cause I might not be there." Yeah, she knows it's my job, and that's what I get paid to do. You work for a utility company and you got to go through all the bad times. That's why you doing the kind of job you're doing.

I don't know if it's great [to be fifty-five years-old]. I'd like to see the guy that says life begins at forty; I'd kill him. This year, Martin Luther King Day, this past January, I saved nine people in a house fire on Euterpe Street. Me and my two men. I busted the doors and the house was on fire and I went upstairs and got them out of bed and save them. The American Gas Association had us come up to Chicago to accept a meritorious award for saving human lives, and a few months later this other gas association recognized us for the same award. So this year was a tough year for me. But yeah, I be glad after December 31 when this year's over with.

[Showing photos of Katrina's aftermath.]

This is a boat like up on top of somebody's car. Now this house here, you can see it's in the middle of the street. The whole house. See where the water level is up here? This is North Tonti Street off of Franklin Avenue. I was trying to find a vacant lot where this house came from. There wasn't no vacant lots. The house actually came a block and a half around the corner and that's where it settled down. That's what's written: "Dead Body Inside." That was in the Ninth Ward. I didn't work too hard that day.

This is by the London Avenue Canal. It looked like a desert because the helicopters were dropping the big sand bags, missing the break and dropping it in the neighborhood. You couldn't hardly see the streets. Some of them you couldn't hardly see the tops of the houses. There's so much sand when you ride through there the sand [covers] half of the cars and everything.

I met a man on Chef Highway, down there, big shrimp boat in the road. Him, his wife, his daughter stayed. He's a fisherman. They stayed in their raggedy, two-story house they had there, and the tornado hit the house and he had to get out. He took his mama, his mama was 79, and the daughter, didn't tell how old, across the road because the water was starting to get up, and he tied his mama in the tree and his daughter. And then next thing, wife come floating by on a door that belonged to the house. He saw her leave. He said he didn't know where she was going to end up. And he said, "It was something to see my mama going back and forth in that tree." But he said, "I had to tie her good. She's a tough old woman. She did really good in that tree." He said the wind took his daughter's clothes off, actually off. After everything calmed down, he went to look for his wife, and he found her back over there in that marsh with all kind of debris on her. I asked him, "Was she alive?" He said, "Yeah, she was fine." He said there was some baby nutria up in the debris with her. And he says, "She's in the camper right here in the trailer." I said, "Are you going to leave?" He says, "I'm a fisherman. That's the only thing I know how to do. I got to stay. I got to stay and make a living." And I got to thinking about that poor mama, 79. Now if the water had been getting higher and higher, even though you had her tied real good, she might not been able to get loose and then you would have drowned your mama. But he didn't think of that at the time. He said, "I have her tied real good. I had them both tied real good, in that tree."

I met a man other night, Baltimore business man, and he says he never met people like down here. They could laugh even after all this tragedy; they could laugh and rebuild. They gonna rebuild. It's no big thing. Most states, they'd still be, they'd panic or a nervous wreck. That's people here. It's like, "It happened, and let's get on with it." I said that's the way it is with people down here. It ain't that they don't take it seriously. They figure, "Hell, it's over with. Let's move on."

But I ain't gonna do it again. Know that.

Have you had bad dreams?

Only dreams I ever had was from Vietnam, but that's so long ago. But not because of the storm.

At one point I was ready to cry because of the storm. I mean my wife had two strokes this past year, and my mother-in-law was with us, and she was supposed to have back surgery the week of the hurricane, but they had to cancel it. Reason they canceled it was her doctor had a heart attack. I told her, "Thank God he did because he could have been operating on you then had a heart attack." She just had surgery two weeks ago, but it was scheduled right before the hurricane, the week of the hurricane, and she had to wait another two or three months to get her surgery.

I mean after the hurricane, we didn't have no water, three grown ups and can't flush the toilet, got two bathrooms. I got to thinking, "Well, my neighbors got a swimming pool and the fence is blown down and I'm looking over there at that pool." That water was crystal clear. So I went with five-gallon buckets. I told her [my neighbor] when she come back, "Danielle, I was stealing your water out of your pool. I had to flush my toilets." She said, "That's all right." Yeah, I had some friends in the neighborhood like four or five blocks away, a couple buddies, they stayed. And it was like a ghost town. We'd come visit each other during the day, the day after the storm, and after it passed. Nobody around, trees, power lines, poles down. And then they found out I had water to flush the toilets. They were coming by with trucks with buckets and we were filling up their buckets so they could flush the toilets, and then we all heard the levees were breaking. Then we all decided, all of us, to go, so we all packed up. We all went different directions but everybody out.

Did you lose anyone?

No. We did have one guy work for us in New Orleans East. He called on the radio, he told them him and his family was in the attic, please come get them, and they said, "Matt, we can't get to you. It's already flooded out there." And then a little bit later he called back and he says, "Look, I made a hole in my roof, me and my family." And he was at the point of crying, saying, "Please somebody, y'all come get me." And they said, "Matt, we can't. Our hands are tied. There's no way we can even get to you." And then a little while later he called back and the last transmission they heard, he says, "I can't hold on no more." And it was almost a month and we thought he drowned. He showed up, he called. He was in Arkansas in the hospital for prostate cancer. Somebody had saved him, and he ended up in Arkansas, and that's where he was getting his treatments, his chemo and all in Arkansas. And we thought for sure he was done, and we'd never see, that him and his family drowned, but some kind of way somebody saved him. He ended up in Arkansas, and he's back at work.

And then we had a few of them we didn't hear from for two or three weeks, so we had no idea whether they alive or whether they dead, but some of them [were] like in Tennessee or here and there. They didn't actually know where we were going to be, so they called. I guess the website said we were stationed in Baton Rouge. Then they started calling to say, "Hey, we OK, and I'll get there whenever I can."

My buddy I was in Vietnam with lives in Texas. And he called the day of the hurricane and says, "Why you didn't come over up in Texas by my place? I been telling you for a week to come." I says, "I'll be all right." Well he talked to me day of the hurricane. After the levees broke, I left. Well he tried calling my house cause the phone was the only thing I still had working and when he didn't get no answer, he thought I flooded and drowned. And I have some relatives in Kentucky felt the same way. They didn't know what happened. They were talking to me the day of the storm, and then they couldn't get in touch with me. And one of my cousins said, "Wayne, he's a survivor. If anybody will make it, he will make it."

Well my buddy in Texas didn't know how to find me or where, if I was alive or if I was dead. But he went through the website, the net. He found some kind of Entergy website, and about a week or so later at the Custom House on Canal Street, the big Custom House, the manager of the gas company, Entergy, calls me. He says on the radio, "Can you call me by phone?" I thought I got in some kind of trouble, so I right away called him. And he says, "You know a Kenny and Sherry Waters in Franklin, Texas?" I said, "Yeah, I was in Vietnam with Kenny Waters." He says, "Please call this guy. He done went through the web. He don't know whether you alive or dead, so please. I got his number. You call him to let him know you alive."

Yeah, like I said, I won't stay no more. Sure it looks a lot better there [in the photos] than it did when you were actually right there. I'm just sorry I didn't get a black and white camera, had everything in black and white. That would have been really good. I'm fine. I just need time off.

Didn't You Hear?

Amber Green
Interviewed by Carol McCarthy

Amber Green was a fourth-grader living in Lakeview when her family had to evacuate to Texas. She talks about her impressions of the storm, her new school, and sharing a room with her sister.

My daddy said that we could not return to New Orleans because the police were working on fixing the city up for kids. I know that there were kids still there because I saw them crying on the TV.

I liked my new school in Texas because we could wear whatever we wanted. Mommy took me on a long shopping trip to buy lots of underwear and jeans and shirts. I got mostly pink shirts because pink is my favorite color. My room has pink walls and a poster of Britney Spears on it.

Which room is pink?

My room. In *my* house. I like my room because I don't have to share it with my bratty sister. I swear I wanted to pull her hair all the time in Texas because she was always crying at bedtime, and we were sharing a bed. I kept telling her to stop crying and stop being a baby. She's only five, but she acts like a little baby. My teacher at school had a baby and brought her in to show us all. All she did was sleep. But not my big baby sister. She never wanted to sleep. Just cry. All the time. I told my mommy, and she said I should be patient or something like that. I learned to fall asleep with my fingers in my ears every night, like I do when there is a lot of thunder and lightening and rain. I hate thunder.

Tell me about your new school in Texas.

Well, I could wear whatever I wanted. And it was good because school was easy there. I am in the fourth grade, and they were only doing simple math, and I was learning about the three M's at my old school. You know, medium, mode, and something else. What was the other one, Mom?

Tell me about the kids in Texas.

They were real nice. I made one friend, Jenna, who let me sleep over at her house a few times. She lived by the school. Some nights her mommy would bring me to school after I slept over. Those nights were real nice because Jenna didn't cry like my stupid sister.

Jenna and I would play with Barbie. She let me play with her Barbies since I didn't bring my own. Her mom even bought me one. I thought it was nice, although I had the same one at home. I took it anyway because then I would have twin Barbies.

Why do you think you were in Texas?

Because of the hurricane. It made the city really wet. God made it rain a lot for almost a week. Didn't you hear? At the new school, the one where I wore jeans, we talked about rain and storms. Some stupid kid in my class said that the rain caused lots of people to die. I asked my Mom if that was true, and she said that the flood caused people to die, not the rain. My grandma died when I was little, but not from flood. She died from cancer. On her birthday we go to the cemetery to give her flowers and pray.

Were you afraid at your new school?

On the first day, I was scared because this one kid on the block we were staying on said I talked funny. He talked funny, not me. I was scared that other kids were gonna make fun of me. I don't think I talk funny. Jenna didn't think I talked funny, either. No one knew I was from New Orleans unless they asked me. I thought the teacher would tell everyone, but she didn't. When I got to school the first day, the teacher said I changed schools. She didn't say I was from New Orleans.

What do you think it means to say that you are from New Orleans?

Oh yeah, it means that I like red beans and rice and that my dad likes music, so I like music. I play the violin and my mom plays the accordion. We go to concerts on Sundays because we all like music. We don't usually play out front of our house because New Orleans is dangerous at night. We play in our backyard at night. We played out front in Texas a lot! It was fun.

Have you seen your pink room since you've been back?

No, daddy says that the police are still trying to clean up the water. I saw a picture of my room, and the water made the walls a little black with spots. He said they have to wash the walls before I can go get my toys. But I haven't had much time to play since my best friend is still with her aunt in Shreveport. And I don't want to play with my stupid sister. She doesn't know how to play with dolls like I do.

This Could Happen Again Next Year

Marjorie and Ralph Guidry
Interviewed by Kristin Schwartz

Marjorie and Ralph Guildry are in their late forties and lost their home in Chalmette. Their grief was compounded by news that Marjorie's father had died overseas shortly after the storm.

Tell me about what you saw on the way home and about what your thoughts were as you got closer to your town, and then, eventually, your house.

Ralph: As we got to Slidell, we started to see some of the [downed] trees. And with damage that far out in Slidell, in the back of my mind I knew what was to come.

Marjorie: All the blue roofs…. And then when we got to my friend in the Crossgates, we began to see all [the debris] at the curbside.

Ralph: It had already been a month, so people had started to clean up. This is when we were in Slidell. I think we had to take Highway 11. I can't remember when we made it back, but what happened is, her father died.

Marjorie: We got here that Thursday, the next day was Friday, and we get word that my father died. For some reason, we didn't bring my passport and couldn't get it. That was Friday. Because of [Hurricane] Rita, they closed St. Bernard again. But anyway, I already had my tickets to get to my brother's in Rhode Island and then to go to Boston, so we could fly to the Philippines. Ralph dropped me off at the airport, and that's when St. Bernard opened.

So I wasn't with him, and that was the first time he saw the house.

Ralph: I was going down here on I–10, they call it Paris Road, and when you get on the top of the Green Bridge, you can see the entire Orleans

Parish and St. Bernard Parish. And I go on top of that bridge and all I saw was water.

There was still water there?

Ralph: What happened there was that there was no more marsh in St. Bernard Parish... This is because of the tidal surge, the storm surge. All water, it was all water. And then when I got down from the bridge... they had several boat places where you launch your boats and buy boats... and all I saw was boats.

Any buildings?

Ralph: I saw buildings. I got past the police checkpoint, and you saw the buildings that were inside the levee system... the bottom part was basically blown out. They had tug boats and barges that were sitting on top of the levees. All you saw was mud everywhere on the streets... and the few main streets they had was clear and the street we had to travel on was the main street... I went down Paris Road, and all you saw each side was damaged properties, flooded cars and mud. And when I got to the street that turns out on Genie [...] on either side there was still mud on the streets, except for the one I was traveling on. And then when I got down to Genie, which is where our street is, that was cleared. So I was kinda fortunate. There were very few that were able to get to their houses before the streets were cleared. At that time, the parish started making an effort to clear the streets so people could get to their houses. The thing was that my house was hardly damaged.

Really?

Ralph: So when I went to the front door, I had my keys, and I was able to unlock it, but I couldn't push the door open. I guess there was stuff blocking it. So I went around to the side door, and when I walk in.... I thought maybe they came here looking for bodies, because that's what they were doing at the time. I said I don't even see the door anymore; the door isn't even here anymore. You have your couch; dining table and TV. Everything was all messed up. I mean we had over nine feet of water.

Over nine feet?

Ralph: Over nine feet. I had anywhere from two inches to eight inches of mud, depending on where you went in the house. I had a TV set that was in the main room; well, somehow it ended up in our bedroom. We eat a lot of rice, and we had big storage boxes, and I didn't know what happened to them. What happened was they ended up in our bedroom.

The rice did?

Ralph: Yeah. We had a king size bed that weighed over 400 pounds, and it was underneath the bed. The bed propped up by the rice storage bins.

Marjorie: Our house was intact, you see? [She shows a picture of the exterior of her house].

Ralph: I think this is the flood line [he points up near the roof in the picture].

Marjorie: You see these houses [showing a picture of her street]... you can see how the water got in there, but look at how intact it is. My car was on the driveway... but see, it washed over to the house. This is the inside. [Shows a picture of the interior of the house]

Ralph: All the cabinets fell down from the water.

Marjorie: This is the only ceiling that didn't come down...Notice all this insulation that came out. So when you look up, you won't see this [gestures to ceiling] anymore. You just see the wood, the frame.

Ralph: The weight of the water, on the ceilings... it's just sheetrock.

Marjorie: And then this, this is our master bedroom right here [gestures to photo]... and this table was in the living room, but it got stuck right here at the bathroom door.

Yeah you can see some of the mud.

Marjorie: You had to make a way just to get inside the house. See how big that table is? The dining table, it floated [shows a picture of an upside down dining table]… and see that? That is ceiling that all came down.

Was there anything salvageable?

Ralph: No furniture. The only piece of furniture is this [very small side table in his house]. That's it. No furniture.

Marjorie: When I got back [from the Phillipines], he said, "Are you ready to see the house?" I think by that time, I was ready. Although I knew the house got flooded…. The only regret I have is not bringing our wedding album. The only thing! Before anything happens, I thought they were gonna burn the house or bulldoze it, if I could just get that or if I could get something before that. Maybe I could just see the house before they do anything. You know, like maybe saying goodbye. That's all I was asking. Our albums that was like in our buffet table. We have traveled a lot.

Ralph: We got a lot of albums. We've been to Europe and….

Marjorie: The things we have from when, you know, we were not married yet, like cards that we sent to each other and like our wedding album, we put that in a plastic bag, and he said put that on like the highest part of the house. I think it got punctured or something, but whatever I could save, I put in water and then let them dry. But the first time I saw the house, I was happy I was able to see it and retrieve some of the stuff, and for me, I was happy about it. I mean, we can't do anything. We have to start all over again.

Ralph: When we came back here, our first night I wanted to take a shower. We had no shower curtain. [laughs]

Marjorie: And I want to cook, and I say, "Oh you have to go to the store." Because you just take for granted things like the cutting board. I don't have a sharp knife. My god, all the things you just… a chopping board to just… I cannot cut. I said we cannot do this; we have to go to the store.

Ralph: When we first got here, we went out all the time and…

Marjorie: So I would go around and write down what we need. It is little things, like the stapler you want to staple papers with or the scissors. You know, those are the little things you need, but they're not there.

What are your opinions about rebuilding, about the town you lived in? What do people that you know that live there think?

Ralph: The girl across the street from me, she used to work at Murphy Oil. She was head of the information department, the computers. She got a job in North Carolina; she quit her job. The guy to my left, he was some kind of manager I guess with A&P or Sav-A-Center; they provided a job for him in Massachusetts. The people across the street from us—he's a mechanic for Mercedes-Benz—they moved to Tennessee.

Marjorie: They got an apartment, and FEMA provided them with rent, a washer/dryer, refrigerator and the people there bought them their furniture. They didn't even buy it! I mean, they have everything. Even better furniture than they had in their house before.

Ralph: The thing with us going back out there is that fixing the levees to the way they were is unacceptable because this thing could happen next year, and we were traumatized by it.

Marjorie: I don't want to go back in that house and every day think about what happened. I mean, I still love my house, but you gonna be there every day, and bad things gonna happen again, and….

Ralph: I could see myself—I'm a little of the nervous type—every time they'd have a hurricane in the Gulf of Mexico, I'd… I'd be, I'd have an anxiety attack. I just don't want to go through it again. Our neighborhood is a wasteland. I don't foresee them having electricity or gas for a long time. They aren't going to get gas for a long time. The gas provider said in an article that some areas may take three months to two years to get gas. They're not going to provide utilities or gas to an area where no one's going to come back to. So far I haven't heard any…. Not too many people are coming back. The only people that are coming back to St. Bernard are those people that have too much to lose.

What Was in That Water?

The Dawson Family
As Told by Amy Ferrara-Smith

As Faith Dawson and her mother work together to clean out their flooded house, they recover few possessions.

Faith and Andonicia Dawson stood armed with a can of WD-40 and a wooden broom in front of their New Orleans East house. The outer gate that protected the front door for 33 years was corroded, stubbornly fastened as a result of the contaminated floodwaters that climbed up the iron and above the threshold to the roof, nearly eight feet from the ground. She and her mother needed a crow bar, Faith thought, something to pry apart the metal, so they could then push through the wooden front door, two small women hoping to retrieve something, maybe just memories, from the house.

From her mother's lifeless front lawn, Faith petitioned passersby for the tool. It wasn't the typical Saturday crowd driving down Chantilly Drive. Instead, animal rescue vans and a few curious onlookers, possibly neighbors, afraid to venture from the seat of their cars and into their houses, drove quietly past the Dawsons, shaking their heads. Finally a car stopped. The man, a local contractor, had a tire iron, and it wasn't long before he realized he was a relative of the Dawsons, a cousin who lived down the street. "Only in New Orleans," Faith laughed later.

For over an hour Faith and Andonicia had a small family reunion at 4824 Chantilly Dr. with Raymond Bonet and his girlfriend as Raymond tried to pry the iron gate open. It was as if the gate was trying to protect them from what lay inside. Faith suggested that he give up, but the girlfriend assured her that'd he be there until he got that gate open, even if it took him until the next hurricane.

Still looking for a crow bar, Faith flagged down an All State Insurance truck that passed by the house. The two men inside hesitated to help, but Faith begged and assured them that she was an All State customer. They obliged wearily.

Raymond moved aside and one of the men, a heavyweight, pushed his body against the iron and broke through the gate. The wooden door was easier. It accepted the key and after a shove, it opened.

Faith hadn't been inside her childhood home in a month, since she had driven from her own house off Esplanade Avenue to pick up her mother for their evacuation to Baton Rouge. She had been shopping for a present that day, which she planned to bring to a friend's engagement party that evening, but when she tried to maneuver through thick traffic lines and saw people mounting plywood to their windows, she thought twice about buying the gift and called her mother.

Not long after, she walked inside the New Orleans East one-story house carrying a small tote bag of clothes and a leash attached to her hundred-pound German Shepard. It took her mother, Faith said, until ten that evening to go through the chain of family communication to see where their relatives would evacuate. Some went to Houston, others to Lake Charles, and a few ended up in Birmingham at a house with twenty other people lodged inside. The Dawsons drove to Baton Rouge to Faith's friend's mother's house, which became more and more crowded with evacuees every day. At that house they heard Katrina had passed over the city, and later they learned that she had caused several levees to break, flooding many neighborhoods in and around Orleans Parish, including New Orleans East. "When the levees broke, my heart broke with them," Faith later said.

In all of this, one of the first things Andonicia lamented about was a $15 white beaded purse that she had bought from a street vendor in New York City while on a mother-daughter trip with Faith. She was proud of that purse, Faith said, and whenever someone complimented it she advertised,

"Streets of New York. 15 dollars."

They stayed for five days in Baton Rouge, and when they heard the roads were clear of debris on the Northshore, the two women drove to Madisonville to stay with Andonicia's sisters, although electricity wouldn't be restored to the area for several days.

But Faith, the managing editor for several publications at MCMedia, LLC, including *New Orleans Magazine*, quickly got what she called "cabin fever" in Madisonville. So when her boyfriend, Donald Costello, invited her to meet him at his mother's house in Boston. Faith was relieved. Andonicia, however, was worried that while Faith was gone, New Orleans would allow residents to return to their homes and everything would be back to normal. It would be another three weeks before they were actually allowed to see their house.

From September 8-15, Faith acted as a tourist, but even 1,500 miles away she couldn't escape her New Orleans identity. Because the line in the northern city was so short, she quickly got her $300 financial assistance money from the Red Cross, and when Bostonians asked her where she was from, they offered her supplies and condolences.

When MCMedia, LLC, opened a temporary office in Port Allen, Faith returned to Louisiana to go back to work. Donald, an ophthalmologist at Ochsner Hospital's Westbank clinic, stayed in Boston for several more days, and Faith worried that he wouldn't return, that he would stay in a place that had modern conveniences, such as passable roads, water services and electricity.

But he did return, and because his house in uptown New Orleans didn't have power yet, the hospital offered him a room in the downtown Sheraton Hotel, which, according to Faith, was "command central" for post-Katrina operations. When she visited, she saw the inner workings of a city, her city, trying to pull itself up out of the floodwaters and onto dry land again, and she felt proud to call herself a New Orleanian. She wanted to stay there, too, to see how this would all come together, to be with people who were also suffering from loss and disbelief, but who shared a pride that went beyond the old French Quarter facades to the local spirit itself.

It was a similar spirit that walked with her through her childhood home, now caked in filth and filled with broken pieces of furniture, as if someone had lifted and shaken it like a snow globe. At one time, when she was a student at Mount Carmel Academy, Faith hated her house. She wanted to move to a "cooler" neighborhood, some place like Uptown, where she thought that she might have a truer New Orleans experience. But in the aftermath of Katrina, while it stood beaten and bruised, Faith felt as though her house was a "being," something that had lived with her throughout her life. It had kept her safe, warm, and dry, and now it had suffered what Faith called an undeserved indignity because of the way she defamed it in her adolescent years. So when Faith's uncle called to tell her to leave the door to her house open when she and Andonicia left in order to air it out, she shut it behind her anyway. It was a private place, a place where she and her mother and her father had created memories, and she couldn't allow herself to carelessly leave it available to the public, as if she didn't respect the same walls that had always guarded her family. No one else in the world would mourn the house except the two Dawsons, she said, but they still felt that it deserved a respectful burial.

Behind that closed door, Faith and Andonicia had trampled over displaced and broken furniture and their kitchen refrigerator, which had fallen over and slid into the living room. Faith's father, who passed away when she was 21, was a jazz aficionado. They found his treasured record collection broken and covered in filth on the floor. But a crucifix, a Madonna portrait, and a statue of the Blessed Virgin Mary were all unscathed among the litter in the house.

People had warned Faith to be prepared for the smell in the rotting house, but she said it was manageable as a kind of organic odor. Nonetheless, with masks and boots on, she and her mother waded through the debris. Faith browsed through a closet where she stored her winter clothes each year and noticed that a sweater had changed from black to red. She later laughed, "What was in that water?"

When they had seen enough of the destruction, Faith walked out of the house, carrying a few salvageable items, among them Andonicia's white satin beaded purse. Faith had retrieved it for her mother before the two women flagged down Raymond to help them open their front door. When they had first arrived at the house, Faith and Andonicia had gone to the backyard to see if they could climb inside through one of the broken windows. They peered into the bedroom and sitting on a mattress that had been lifted to a 45-degree angle was the small white purse in a plastic bag, untouched. Faith stuck a broomstick into the bedroom and lifted the bag outside, as if fishing in a murky swamp.

What they didn't find in the house was Dakota, Faith's nine-year-old German Shepherd. In their post-Katrina visit, they learned for the first time that the neighbor across the street had been keeping 72 pets, and when the hurricane threatened the area, she abandoned them in the house. 53 of them died and 19 survived. Maybe Dakota was as lucky as those 19 and was safe somewhere in a shelter or an adopted home.

After she said goodbye to her house and to the memories within it, Faith changed her email address. She is now FaithinNola@xxx.com, and while she helps her mother to physically rebuild what she lost, Faith will be one of the many locals who returns to her hometown to prove that the spirit of New Orleans thrives, not only in the buildings of the city, but in the hearts of the locals who are restoring them.

What Are We Going to Do With These Old People?

Third Street, Kenner, LA
As Told to Mary Sparacello

After the storm, Fred Duncan turned his looted grocery store, Duncan Food Mart, into an impromptu emergency shelter, housing senior citizens who lived previously in a nearby apartment building known affectionately as the "old folks' home," which was destroyed during the hurricane. John Peyton, 64, spends his nights at Duncan Food Mart and his days at his old apartment, where he sits in a plastic chair facing River Road. Ernestine Wells, 80, spent Hurricane Katrina in a LaPlace hospital. Upon release, she moved into the Duncan Food Mart with her neighbors. She now lives with her niece but still spends her days at the store. Julia Ralle LeRoux, 56, was sent to the makeshift shelter by the American Red Cross, but there were no beds left. She still spends her days at the Food Mart and attempts here to dispel the rumor that she sleeps under an interstate bridge in St. Rose at night.

Fred Duncan

We left the day before the hurricane. We had seven carloads of people—my grandmother, grandfather, sister, wife, daughters—all family members. We had a hotel outside Memphis and stayed there for about two days. From there we went to Utica [Mississippi], to the casino. They said there was free rooms out there. We stayed there three or four days. When we got back on the road we had five carloads. Kin folk was telling us to go to Chicago. They had rooms and everything set up for us. We stayed there for about a week. My uncle and aunts live in Indiana, so we left Chicago and headed to Indiana. We dropped some people off in Chicago. When we left there, we were only two carloads. We stayed there for about a week. In the meantime, my daughter lives in Detroit, so we headed to Detroit. We stayed there three days until we headed home because my other daughter left her new car at home. We had seven cars in our driveway at home; we were lucky none of them flooded. When we came back here to get her car, we had to get special permission to get back in. We took [my daughter's] car back to

Detroit. We stayed up there another three days.

Where we were living at [in Detroit] they were building FEMA trailers to send this way. Thousands of trailers that I knew they would put on vacant land in Kenner. I said, "We got to get back. We got to get back." When I did get back I saw they done looted my whole store, took my back door off. It was cleaned out. They had taken everything, cigarettes, all the cool drinks. The freezer was empty. They tore an iron gate down and came through two iron doors.

But then I saw the apartments next door. I went into a couple of their apartments, and it was raining on their heads. I said to the city councilman, "What are we going to do for these people with no roof? You know I got a couple of buildings from people who hadn't come back." The councilman told me, "You can't put people in a commercial building without getting certification from Kenner." But I said, "Let's bite the bullet and do what we have to do." I said, "You all come over here." People were calling me saying they need a place to stay, their homes got flooded. I had 15 or 16 people over there. The City of Kenner called and asked me, "Why do you have a shelter open over there? It's not certified." I said, "What are we going to do with these old people? Will you take care of them?" They never messed with me after that. We still got five people in the shelter from the storm.

We have beds, a shower. They come here to eat. It's just like a bed and breakfast basically. The American Red Cross is sending me people, and I'm not a certified shelter. It's three or four times that the [Red Cross] shelter has sent over people. I can't take anyone else in.

John Peyton

Before the storm, I bought cold drinks or hot breakfasts at the store. Now, I sleep there at night. I know it ain't going to last forever. I stayed in my room during the storm, up there on the third floor. When Katrina started shaking the building, I drove in my pickup to Bonnabel [local high school used as a shelter]. After it started shaking my room, it mostly ripped off the roof. That's when I drove to the school. There were a lot of people there; I didn't know them. There were people there from the city.

I drove back here after Katrina. Mr. Frank [the landlord] let me move to the first floor where it don't get wet. People came around with food every day. The American Red Cross came in a van and took us to the City Hall to get a debit card. Maybe a week ago, maybe 10 days. I got about $300 to buy gas with. I ride around in my pickup. They come by in the van a lot and give us food pretty much every day. Freddie [Duncan] also gives us food. They're nice.

A month and a half after Katrina, the "old folks' home" looks deserted. Flies hover above scraps of food, styrofoam boxes, empty bottles, and cigarette cartons. The area in front of the complex is almost as messy as Peyton's third-floor apartment, where fluffy pink insulation peeks out from the walls and the ceiling exposes a view to the sky. Peyton's clothes sit in a moldy stack on the floor.

This is my room up here. I couldn't save anything. Katrina blew off the roof and the rain came in. I try and sweep the rain out when it comes. I keep some clothes in my truck. Some clothes the Red Cross give me. A few people still live here, in their apartments. I don't know why they don't go live at the food store. I come here during the day to see my friends. They're not really living here. They're surviving here.

Ernestine Wells

I live with my niece right now. I ain't got nowhere to stay. I'm staying with her. I was in the hospital during the storm. I was sick, but I didn't know what was wrong with me. When I bent over to my shoes I said, "There's a hurt right there." It's gallstones.

Was I scared? No, I wasn't scared. Well, I was scared, but I couldn't do nothing about it. That's the Lord's way. I don't know nothing because I was in the hospital. I didn't see nothing; I don't know nothing. All I know I was in LaPlace, in the hospital.

It was over there, next door, that they came and got me. Edgar, that boy, I don't know where he at now. He came and got me out and took me to a shelter. I lived at 1039 Third Street right there, Apartment B1. I been living at 1039 a long time. I didn't want to go, but he said, "It's raining on you.' [Whispering] It wasn't raining on me; it was raining in the next bedroom. Edgar. I don't know where he's at.

I stayed at the shelter till my niece came and got me from there. She live on Plantation Drive [a mile away]. She take good care of me, cooks for me. They had roof damage, but it's fixed now. She brings me here in the morning. I ain't supposed to walk in the heat. I ain't supposed to cook. That's the Lord's will, and I can't do nothing about it.

Julia Ralle LeRoux

I was living in a third-floor apartment on West Napoleon Avenue in Central City. I live alone, just myself. Friday afternoon (before the hurricane) I went home. I stayed there until the hurricane. It was Category 4 and 5 winds, I saw on TV, 150-mile winds. Lots of wind and water. It was a big storm. I was staying in the hallway because the wind might blow something through my window. I just put pillows on the floor and a blanket. It was a shelter in the hallway.

I stayed there until Tuesday morning, and then I left. The street was flooded up to the bottom step of my apartment building. I walked to the CBD [the Central Business District in downtown New Orleans, where buses were headquartered, a three mile walk]. Once I got on a bus on Canal Street, it took me two days to get to a shelter. I went with a group of people to Lafourche Parish. I went to Nicholls State University. I was there three days. A very nice place there, a beautiful campus.

My cousin in Atlanta called me; he came to Nicholls to get me. I stayed with him for six weeks in a four-bedroom home in Atlanta. I got back to

New Orleans on Southwest Airlines. I came back and went to Baton Rouge, to the Jimmy Swaggart Baton Rouge College, to a residence hall there. That's where I stayed in November and December. Then I came back from Baton Rouge, on a bus on Highway 61.

I retired as a nurse. I'm retired from employment since March. I should have a retirement check. I have to check my mailbox; it's on Williams. I'm really on my way to St. Rose right now, going to take a city bus to St. Rose, past St. Rose. Am I homeless? No, I'm all right. I've got a place. I may not be here for too long. I'm probably going to live here for another year. I'm not sure yet. I'm staying with friends right now, but I haven't really decided where I'm going to stay for the next year. I'm waiting for Monday. When I get the mail from my Post Office box, I'll see if my retirement check is there. When I get it, I will rent an apartment like my apartment on West Napoleon. I don't want something big, just something for me. I want a small room for one.

Everything Is Scattered

Mary Fleetwood
Interviewed By Eileen Guillory

Mary Fleetwood is an 85-year-old New Orleans native who lived in Gentilly Woods for 46 years until Katrina took her home. She describes the difficulties of starting over at 85. She is interviewed here by her granddaughter.

Could you describe your experience during hurricane Betsy?

Well, it was very stressful. Years ago, we didn't know anything about evacuating. We didn't use those words. [For Hurricane Betsy] we thought it would be best to be with our relatives, and my husband's mother had a home in the vicinity, and it was raised. So we thought that we'd all be together so we took our dog and left our home, and we went [to my mother-in-law's]. That was the most stressful, one of the most stressful, nights of my life. The wind was howling. And the debris! Things were hitting the roof. [It was] coming off and [the] tin was hitting the house and, and we, well, we prayed all night and stayed up. And the next morning, when we opened the door, we saw—we never had experienced that before—water in the streets up to almost our waist. Our car was gone. It was flooded, and so we decided we [had] better get home and check our house. So the dog and my husband and I left, and we walked through the waters until we got to an underpass, and the water was very deep there. They had other people besides us, children, and of course it would have been over their heads. So they had police patrols, and they were pulling [us] up over the [train] trestle. And then, we got to the other side where it was a lot lower, because of course, we were away from the underpass. And then, the waters were receding; and, we got near my home—it's about 20 miles, I mean, 20 blocks away. They had to walk and the dogs had to swim through all of this. When we got to my home, it seemed to be spared. There didn't seem [to be] anything but some little tree limbs around, which we were thankful for, but we did have some repercussions, because my husband had suffered from ulcers, and he had bleeding ulcers after this and was hospitalized. Seriously. And my dog, the little pet dog, died two days later, from heart failure, the vet said. So all this was an aftermath of Betsy.

How did this experience during Betsy affect your perspective on hurricanes? How did you view hurricanes?

Well, it made us more aware of how serious they were because that was the first experience we ever had with a hurricane so we [didn't] know how devastating it could be because we did have a few people die in this particular hurricane, and some of them died in our area. They were trapped. They got to their attics, and they couldn't get out. Years ago, they didn't— elderly people—they didn't have hatchets and [they] just couldn't go through the roof.

When did you evacuate from New Orleans for Katrina?

We decided to evacuate two days before Katrina because—years ago, we were in our 40's for Betsy—we just thought it was best to go to my daughter's home. She lives in a rather safe area in Hammond, and, since I hadn't been driving in my old age, and [my] husband had a stroke and was ailing, my granddaughter, Eileen, picked us up, and she drove us to my daughter's home.

So Hammond, Louisiana, is about an hour away?

Yes, it is. It's an hour.

Did you know of any help that was offered to you by the government or by nonprofit organizations to evacuate during Katrina? Was there any help given to evacuate the elderly before Katrina that you know of?

Well, we didn't hear of anything, and ah, we just decided to do it on our own. Ah, we lived in what they call the Westside of the Industrial Canal, and we had cars. Now, maybe they had [information] on the radio, which we did not have on this particular time. They might have had something saying for people that didn't have cars, that they could gather in some certain areas, but we were not aware of anything like that.

After the storm passed in Hammond, how were you able to get your medications or other necessities to survive?

Well, after the storm passed and I was at my daughter's home, I had only taken medication for a few days because we always thought, like everybody else in New Orleans, that we would be home in a couple of days. So I went to go back home, but it was flooded for weeks and they wouldn't even let us go back to check on it. [I asked] Walgreen's if they could refill my medications, and they gave me one pill for my heart and one pill for my high blood pressure, which was not any help at all.

How did you first hear that your home was lost during Katrina?

Well, we heard that on the radio because the TV [was out]. We did have some storm trouble here in Hammond at my daughter's home. It seems like the wind did affect the wires, the power lines, so we had no electricity. And her water comes from a well [with an electric pump], so we didn't have any water.

What items did you lose? What was the damage to your home?

Well, the damage to my home was just about a total loss. [We] lost all of our furniture, our bedding, our linens, but the worst part was we lost some heirlooms. Because we had things a lot of younger people do not have. We had washboards and our old-style irons that people used before they ever had electricity, things that cannot be replaced, and, of course, we lost all our family photos. My mother and my grandmother, they all lived into their 80's, and we lost all of that and wedding pictures of my daughter, which can never be replaced. So we actually had nothing.

Did you have any help salvaging the items from your home?

Well, just the family. Yes, family rallied around. No outside help, just the family. They had to remove all this furniture and muck. They had to scrape it out with shovels, after the police let us in, of course. That was several weeks later. We didn't know what we would find. We were very apprehensive, and then, after that, we had to, what they call, gut the house, and we didn't have any outside help, just my daughter and my son-in-law. He's a good fellow. They helped us.

Were you able to find a few items in your home?

We did find a few items. The water wasn't up to the ceiling, but the water stayed in so long. That's why we lost all the furniture. We did save a few items, but they were nothing. Just a few ornaments that we had, Christmas ornaments, stored up in the lockers high. Nothing really of value.

How has Katrina impacted your life?

Well, my life will never be the same. The worst part about my life now is that it's scattered. My brother was in his 90's. He lost his home in Bay St. Louis, and he had to evacuate to his daughter's home in Dallas, and now he'll probably die in Dallas, and we'll never get—you know—get to see him again. But we're elderly; we just have to talk on the phone. Years ago, I mean before Katrina, we used to visit each other. Bay St. Louis is only an hour and five minutes away from New Orleans. So now our whole life has changed, and now I'm living in one room. Of course, I have the run of my daughter's home. I mean, I can do what I want and fix anything I want. But my possessions are in one room, and it's very crowded and not the same. Nothing will ever be the same, and I lost my husband, too, before Katrina, so it was very devastating to me. I had the stress of losing him plus Katrina.

What do the elderly have to deal with that maybe the younger residents of New Orleans who went through similar experiences may not have to deal with? How is it a unique situation for the elderly?

Well, I think it's because the elderly have more problems with their health, and we were stressed out like younger people would be, too, but we had to worry about trying to get our medications. And as you're older, you don't have, you might say, the bounce that younger people have. You tend to think back on all your memories, and you worry about what happened, and you can't start over; you're too old. I mean, you might try, but in my case I couldn't start over. My husband was gone, and I couldn't go back to New Orleans and live by myself, with my, you might say, my ailments.

So what are you deciding to do with your home?

Well, that's another stressful thing. It's too much uncertainty about my home. I was thinking of waiting for the Road Home recovery program, but that may take months and months because they said there might be up to 80,000 [applicants]. I just know what I read in the paper, and you're not going to get anything for [your home]. That's another reason why I can't rebuild. I had no insurance. I didn't... I never had a drop of water in my home for the 46 years that I lived there, for any hurricane or storm, and we were rather elevated because it was terraced in Gentilly. We had flood insurance one or two years and nothing ever happened so we just figured, well, it's a waste of money, we'd drop it.

Do you think your situation would be different if you were 40 years younger? Would you make the same decisions about your home?

Well, if I was younger I would probably go back because, after all, your roots are in New Orleans if you lived there all your life. You'd want to go back, but if [I] was in my forties, I probably would, because then I would have my husband with me, too. But, like I say, now I have little heart problems and things. You're not going to want to go back and be by yourself.

Was it difficult to move into a different community, when you were accustomed to your grocery store and church?

Well, yes. I miss my church because the pastor was very sincere; we had a little friendship with him. Now, of course, I can't go back; it's too far away.

It's over an hour drive, and since I don't drive, I have to depend on my daughter. Of course, you do miss your friends. They have all scattered. Life is different now. You just have to make the best of it.

Approximately how many years did you attend that church?

I attended that church for the forty-something years. My daughter and all my grandchildren were baptized there, and my daughter was married there.

Overall, can you think of some differences or similarities between hurricane Betsy and hurricane Katrina?

Well, hurricane Katrina was the most devastating one we ever had because the levees broke, and I think everybody realizes now that it was not the rain from Katrina that flooded their homes there. It wasn't the rain from Katrina; it was the flood waters from the levees breaking, and, we didn't just have one levee break, we had four. I live by the Industrial Canal; that's the one that broke by my house, and then they had [one break] in Lakeview, which is another section of our city. They had the 17th Street Canal that broke. And then, of course, they had other canals that overflowed and breaches, so this was the worst. The devastation! The city couldn't.... Of course, maybe I'm predicting it, but it's supposed to be.... Everybody seems to think that it will never be the same, or it will take years, maybe five to ten years, because they still have debris on the curbsides, and people have still not gutted their homes, especially the elderly, because they can't do it. I was just lucky that my son-in-law and family helped out because the elderly can't gut their homes. In fact, the *Times Picayune* had pictures in today's paper of an elderly woman waiting for some church group or someone to come gut her home. And that's a year and several months after Katrina. So if you can't gut your home, how can you go back and live in it? Most people, now, are waiting for this recovery money to redo their homes.

Approximately how many feet of water were in your house?

There seems to be about six feet of water, but what happened was it stayed in there three to four weeks, and that's what did the damage. Because we had mold and we couldn't save the home. The structure was OK.

Was there any experience that stuck out in your mind when you were going to view your home for the first time?

Well, yes. I wanted to find some of our mementos and pictures. I didn't have a lot of jewelry, but I did have some necklaces and chains that were given to me when I was first graduated from high school [at] 18 years of age. And years ago people didn't get diamonds, a lot of diamonds. Nowadays, you give your loved ones diamonds. But there was this tiny little diamond I couldn't find, and my husband had a nice ring with some diamonds that's from when he graduated. Will we finally find that in the muck after digging? The jewelry wasn't that expensive, but it meant something to us. We lost all of that.

Does it ever make you angry or upset when you realize that most of the people that were found dead after Katrina were elderly?

It really upset me because they really had no way of getting out. I'd be in their position, be dead, if I would have stayed because I couldn't get up into the attic by myself. And even if I got into the attic, I couldn't cut through the roof, and most of these elderly people who died, they died in their attics because they couldn't cut through the roof. That's my opinion, and I'm sure that's it because they found their bodies in the attic, and some of them had hatchets and some of them didn't. Some of them just thought they would be rescued in a day or two. Some of them have a few little provisions they had, you read in the paper afterwards, they had a flashlight and some sandwiches or crackers because that was the thing about Katrina: everybody that you talked to said we'll be back in a few days, and that's one of the reasons why a lot of people didn't take their possessions. I didn't take any of the wedding pictures because we just thought we'd be back in a few days. That's the irony of it.

I Hate the City; I Want to Live in St. Bernard

Sue LeBlanc
As Told by Carol McCarthy

Sue LeBlanc grew up in St. Bernard Parish, met her husband in grade school, and lived blocks away from her childhood home until Katrina. At the time of this interview, Sue and her family were renting an apartment in uptown New Orleans.

Going home to survey the damage was not that hard for Sue. When she evacuated with her husband and three kids, she didn't pack like she normally packed. She usually packed the sentimental items, such as baby pictures, wedding albums, birth certificates and the like. And it was a ritual. They have always evacuated for hurricanes since their first child was born, almost seven years ago. She'll never forgive herself for not packing those precious things. In the background, her daughter tells us that Nanna has pictures on *her* wall. Sue reminds her that Nanna, too, was flooded, and her daughter goes back to watching the television in their rented Uptown apartment. I ask Sue if we should go outside and finish talking. She tells me no, that this is reality, and they (her children) are old enough to hear. I admire her courage to talk in front of them, wondering how much they really comprehend about all of this.

Blake, Sue's husband, had been back to the property several times. Sue had been unwilling to go, saying, "What for?" She assumed there was nothing worth looking at. The day she finally decided to go look, they dropped the children off at her sister's house on the Westbank and headed to St. Bernard. The water was still high in a lot of places. They had to park their car blocks away from where they lived because the roads were impassable.

She remembers the clothes she wore that day, a pink Old Navy ball cap, blue jeans, a pink Disney T-shirt, maroon socks, and white tennis shoes. As they walked for blocks toward their house, she remembers the muck and dirt slopped all over the place. She tried to notice some landmark that was familiar to her; there were no street signs up. The trees and grass were dying. She tried not to breathe too deeply, fearing the smell would fill her lungs and belly and cause her to vomit.

She remembers when she first moved in to the house. Blake owned it before they were married, and she often spent the night there. She remembers how it looked then, almost ten years ago, when she wanted to change the color of the walls from bachelor white to shades of yellow and blue. She wanted a new fridge, and she wanted to plant flowers in the front yard.

Sue tells me that Blake never wants to talk about "before," using her hands to make the quotations above her head. She rolls her eyes and tells me that it was awful, but not nearly as frightening as she dreamed it would be. The front door was missing, and she shrieked, asking Blake what happened to it. He told her he had to kick it in to enter the house. Some of the windows were completely gone, and Sue said she wondered if he had also kicked those in or if they broke from the weight of the water. She looked up at the sun that moment and wondered what it must have been like to be submerged to the roof.

She slipped her dust mask on as she walked through the threshold of her front door. She was completely amazed at what she saw. She calls it the rearrangement of her house, chuckling nervously. The kitchen table was in the front room, standing neatly against the curio cabinet that was lying face down. Her sofa was standing up on its side, long ways, and the coffee table was perched up right beside it. The pictures of her children that had hung on the wall above the fireplace were missing. Each eight-by-ten frame had held all the most recent pictures of each child, behind which were all the previous years' photos. "Real wood frames," she tells me. I asked her about the smell, and she raised her eyebrows to remind me that although she had the mask on, she could smell a faint odor.

She had to leave the house. She went back out front for a moment, Blake following in her steps. She said he told her something like, "Sue, it's important that you continue to look at this, for closure." She tells me that she is angry at him for using such a cliché. There would be no closure. There would be no end.

Almost an hour later, she returned to the house and asked if it was OK to walk up the stairs. They all went together to try to see if anything in the attic was all right. Blake opened the attic, and they noticed the mold all over the boxes. The boxes felt moist to the touch, and they were unsure if it was the humidity of the October weather or the moisture left from the flood waters. Blake pulled out one box after another. The boxes farther on in the attic were ones that Sue was hoping were intact, as they contained keepsakes like her wedding dress and her grade-school pictures. She was doubtful, but urged Blake to keep pulling out the boxes. One by one, they carried them down the stairs out to the front yard, not opening a single one until they were all fished out of the attic.

Her fears were confirmed as she noticed the writing on the boxes had faded or melted away. Each box, filled with so many memories, was torn open and searched for one decent thing to salvage. Blake's Matchbox cars from his childhood seemed to be something that could be cleaned and salvaged. Her papers from grade school and high school were mushy and falling apart as she tried to page through them. She stared at the box she knew held her wedding dress and mementos from that date and resolved not to even look in that one. Sue started to cry and asked if I could come back later.

When I came back a few hours later, donuts in hand, I asked her how she was doing. She was on the front porch smoking and shrugged her shoulders. I took the donuts inside to the kids and asked her if she would like to finish.

She said this: "That house, those boxes, that city, that land, defines me. My children know nothing else other than Mommy and Daddy and home. I am that way, too. My momma and papa are in Georgia, livin' in housing given by my momma's job. I haven't seen them in months. I never went away to college, never traveled to no other country, barely made it out of Louisiana except for one trip to Disney Land and to Mississippi to evacuate from hurricanes. I don't know no other life than the one I had in that little house of ours. I grew up there. Went to school there. Lost my virginity in the bedroom of my high school boyfriend three doors down from where I live, or lived until this mess. What am I gonna do? I ain't got no job. My husband has always worked, and I took care of the house and kids. Now I have no house. I don't want to live in New Orleans. I hate the city. I want to live in St. Bernard."

She stopped short and went inside, hearing the kids crash around their two bedroom apartment in Uptown. They were renting it for $1100 per month, a huge difference from their $780 mortgage in St. Bernard. I waited for her to come back out, but she never did.

Like Pockets Turned Inside Out

Echo Olander
As Told to Missy Bowen

Echo Olander is a New York native who directs KidSmart, a program that provides art education and opportunities for children in economically depressed sections of New Orleans. Her home and neighborhood were virtually untouched by Katrina.

October is always the best month to be in New Orleans. The sky is sparkly blue, the air crisp and clear. It's a time of festivals and the cultural season starts to ramp into overdrive. In May, the weather hits the nineties and stays that way through September with the punishing heat and oppressive humidity. October is literally a breath of fresh air, much awaited and rejoiced.

This year the weather is no different; it's the rest of the stuff that is strange. I was away from home for seven weeks and have been back now for two. The sun sparkles, the birds are starting to return, and the butterflies are making their annual trek through this strange and damaged city. There are colossal problems, and the depth and breadth of the damage is astounding.

We live in what I now call the bubble, that lucky area that didn't get any flooding. Almost all the roofs in my neighborhood are covered with blue tarps. They couldn't see the missing tiles on our roof, and we weren't home to watch, so our roof is uncovered though we will probably need a new one. The blue tarps were put on by the National Guard and other military. My neighbor said, "Oh girl, you missed it. Those boys stripped to their pants, with their shoulders and tight stomachs, climbing around every roof in the neighborhood. Girl, we were telling them there's another house right there to do!"

A surprising number of trees and limbs have come down. Many homes took a lot of water through the roof and are being gutted. Just about every refrigerator in the city has been discarded. As the owners were unable to get back to the city, the food festered in the heat, and the smell was impossible to remove from the plastic. When we first returned, all around town you could find these refrigerator conferences, a group of refrigerators hanging out on the street together. They turned into public posting places with people spraying voodoo signs and comments about Saints owner Tom Benson and FEMA's Michael Brown on the doors and sides.

There was a chicken and egg situation here that hasn't completely righted itself. Places can't open and services can't happen if there aren't people to work. People can't work if there aren't places open, services available, and housing. Housing is insufficient to say the least. Many people are waiting to have a place for their children to go to school. Before the storm, there were around 400,000 residents; there are 70,000 now with an estimated 80% of the housing stock damaged.

Upon our return two weeks ago, there were mountains of trash everywhere. People were at their wit's end as the stink of the trash grew stronger. Trash pickup has gotten better; we now have weekly trash pick-up, sort of. As new households return to the city, new mountains of trash grow outside the homes.

During evacuation, we were advised to forward our mail. What they didn't tell us is that it would take another three to five weeks to redirect. We're receiving sporadic delivery, unsure whether there actually isn't any mail (only first class mail is working, so no magazines or second class mail) or whether there is no mailman. The main post office took a load of water and still doesn't have electricity.

Our land line came back on last Friday after we suspended our phone service, and the phone company entered it as a stop order. We still have no internet at home. The sound of a diesel truck brought us running to the front of the house to see who it was. We stopped Entergy to look at the wires and BellSouth to try and get the phone started. The neighbors report chasing trash haulers around the street to try and get them to stop and pick up. You stop anyone in a uniform or hard hat to see if they have a service you might be able to use. We are inundated with flies. These really small ones that look like fruit flies, I've been told, are called coffin flies.

Our school system is bankrupt financially, socially and directionally. The infighting is extraordinary, and the "leaders" struggle with half-assed plan after half-assed plan. A state takeover seems imminent.

That's the good side of town, the lucky side. There's a line, the water line, and when you cross over it, you're not in Kansas any more. In my neighborhood, it starts around Freret Street ten blocks away, twelve from the river. During the day, the neighborhoods look gray and dead. At night, they're pitch black with no electricity. You get in your car and drive and drive and drive and drive, all the way to the Lakefront, across to the East, down to St. Bernard Parish, and all you see are miles and miles and miles of homes that were flooded. In the community center where I work, only myself and two others, out of a staff of about thirty, did not flood.

You can follow the occasional ridge—Esplanade Ridge, Gentilly Ridge— where the ground is higher and the buildings aren't flooded at all. One house will be dry, next house one foot, and the next block will have had four feet. The water line snakes across the buildings as you drive. You find yourself constantly watching to see just how high the water was. People liken it to a brown bathtub ring. It's mesmerizing, watching the line go up and down on the buildings. The water line has stripes, several markings where the water stopped for a while as it was pumped out. Sometimes even the bushes have the stripes on them. All over the place are boats left on the street from when there was water.

All of the houses have a mark that the rescue crews put on as they went from building to building checking for people. Spray painted on the front of the houses are large X's with various codes indicating whether the building looks safe, if they found any bodies inside, if there is electricity down, etc.

On the lakefront, only piers remain of the music clubs and restaurants. One of our favorite places to take visitors for seafood, Sid Mar's, is nothing but piers. There are dead cars everywhere. For every house, one or two cars to go with it: more trash to add to the heap. The amount of trash is unfathomable. I heard a figure today: twenty-two million tons.

To get into their homes, people don face masks, jumpsuits, plastic shrimping boots, and gloves, pulling pile after pile of their belongings on the curb to be thrown away. Thousands and thousands of houses are being emptied like pockets turned inside out. Each building is reviewed to determine whether it is structurally sound and what the insurance covers. Then owners will determine whether they can or should rebuild on the site.

This process takes forever. Because of the water, flood insurance is what covers the losses. If you can prove you had wind damage before the flood, you might have a bit more coverage. If you had a recent mortgage, you were required to have flood insurance if you're in the flood zone. If you owned your house outright, had an older mortgage, or lived outside the flood zone, it was not a requirement, and many people did not have it. Maximum coverage for flood insurance is $250,000, which includes the house and the contents. Many people get less. We spoke to a friend last week who had 18 years equity in the house and recently refinanced. The flood insurance will cover $160,000 on a $225,000 mortgage. The house, recently appraised at $402,000, is a tear-down. After 18 years, the insurance will go to the bank to cover the mortgage and the owner has a lot with no house and a mortgage of $65,000.

If people are rebuilding, the house is stripped to the studs, and the sheetrock, furniture, carpeting, and anything else that was ruined goes to the curb. Many people are trapped as they must wait to find out what their insurance will cover and whether the house is deemed a tear-down or not. Some live on the second floor of their flooded homes while they wait to hear the verdict, as they're tired of living in hotel rooms or on relatives' floors. The government has been unclear about what the new requirements for building are. Are slab foundations permitted? Must houses be elevated? To what level? If they rebuild, when will gas, water, electric services be restarted? It's been over two months and not very many people have the answer to those questions. If the house had flooding, or water from holes in the roof, people are fighting for their lives against the growing mold. Everything is thrown out of the house. The sheetrock is cut to a few feet above the water level, all of the electricity and often the plumbing have to be replaced. With people unable to return, the mold lived in its favorite environment, warm and moist, no air circulating. Homes are covered floor to ceiling with climbing black mold.

In the Lower Ninth Ward, out in the East, and in lower St. Bernard Parish, the jury is still out about whether it is safe to rebuild. Many wait and wait to see what the official edict will be. Between the insurance, talking to FEMA, and trying to ascertain what the city will be doing in those neighborhoods, people are in a frustrating standstill. The waiting is endless and the lack of answers and support from governmental agencies is taxing for the public.

The damaged area extends from western Louisiana to Mobile along the coast. People in Mississippi have been living in tents on their land for months, waiting to hear what will be covered, waiting for FEMA-promised trailers. An article in the Sunday paper said there is no way manufacturers will be able to make as many trailers as have been promised. The state of Mississippi had the storm pass over it for hours, taking trees down and knocking out power all the way up through Laurel, Mississippi, about three hours from here. They are quietly suffering there, and taking in many of the children and their families who were displaced from New Orleans in the storm.

Everyone suffers from some form of posttraumatic stress disorder, touched by overwhelming loss: of the material, of a city, of a culture, of a lifestyle. Returning, you have no idea if the city will be safe enough to live in without strong levee protection, and the variables about how life will be are too many to count. For many, the loss includes a family member, home, job, car, all earthly possessions, or all of the above.

I've taken lately to asking people their story instead of asking how they fared in the storm. How do you ask what all has been lost? A friend who lost absolutely everything wrote me, "What to do, what to do?" You talk to people and they say they did well considering, and they had four feet of water in their house. People comment regularly on the loss of short-term memory, the short attention span, the sleeplessness and the emotional rollercoaster they are on.

We are nervous about the loss of culture, the loss of population, the loss of our Democratic edge in Louisiana. The fear of loss is pervasive and goes as far as the housing stock. We've lost an incredible inventory of plaster and lathe homes with slate roofs. It just goes on and on.

All of that said, the spirit of the city lives on. The people here are extraordinary. Everyone notes that the storm brings out either the best or the worst in people. It has brought out the best in most of the folks I've come in contact with. People just want to be home and they want it to be like it was, only better, and they're working hard to make that happen.

Last weekend was Halloween. Restaurants were bustling and clubs were packed. We went to see the Rebirth Brass Band at Tipitina's. The club was sold out, the crowd excited and happy, dancing their cares away to a rockin' show. To the tune of "Ghostbusters," they sang, "When you're up on your roof, in the neighborhood, who you going to call? Call FEMA." Following a visit to the Maple Leaf to hear the extraordinary Jon Cleary, we headed home laughing and joking. The car quieted as we drove down Freret Street, pitch black on the left side of the car and twinkling lights on the right.

People ask what it is like to be back. And it's kind of like that, a void on one side and some beauty and magic on the other. It's much like having your life be an Advent calendar; each day you open the door and something new is there. But you can't be sure what.

The bubble is beautiful.

Us, Two Dogs, a Cat, and a Bird

I. J. Shelton Jr.
In His Own Words

Lynn and Jud Shelton have permanently relocated to Hiram, Georgia, to be close to their daughter and her family. They feel that there is nothing in New Orleans for them to return to and that they have lost everything except for their memories.

Sunday 8.28.05

The alarm clock rings at 8:00 a.m., and I get up as usual to make coffee and get the Sunday paper from the front porch. I don't bother to shave because I know there won't be any customers at the restaurant where I work as manager. They have all left town ahead of Hurricane Katrina, heeding the call from the mayor to evacuate and having the means to do so.

I take my wife, Lynn, with me to the restaurant, as I often do, so she can visit the shops in the mall nearby, but all the stores and banks have shut down. I call the owner to let her know that we're not staying at work and send the staff home. I raid the walk-in cooler before we leave, so we'll have food at home for a few days. I also take a large ice chest full of ice in case the power goes out. We head back home to watch The Weather Channel and wait for Katrina. With two dogs, a cat and a bird, no cash or credit cards, and a 15-year-old van on its last legs, we have little choice but to hunker down and ride out the storm.

Monday 8.29.05

I awake to the sound of wind and rain lashing the house. Lynn and I watch the storm through the kitchen window as we drink the last pot of coffee we will ever brew in this house. The worst of the storm blows through from 10 a.m. to noon. The only obvious damage is a broken windowpane from a tree branch blown against it. A piece of plastic over the hole stops the water from coming in, and we count ourselves lucky that it wasn't worse.

So much for Katrina. No big deal.

We have no electricity, but that is to be expected. It's time for a nap. We snuggle on the couch in the utility room two steps down from the back of the house. After two hours, we are awakened by a wet cat shaking water all over us. That is when we realize water is entering the house, coming in at the rate of about two inches an hour. We start getting things off the floor and stacking them higher, thinking that the water will stop rising soon. As the water starts to seep through the front door, we realize there is no time to get everything we want to save to a higher place. We only have time enough to get into the attic with the animals, some food for all of us and some water. I spend the rest of the day looking down from the attic watching the water rise. It finally stops at a little under 5 feet. We go to sleep not knowing how we would all get out, but knowing that we would have to somehow.

Tuesday 8.30.05

We wake up to dead quiet all around. There are no birds, no traffic, none of the usual sounds of the city. As the sun starts to rise, I hear the sound of helicopters flying. Then I hear the sound of a boat motor and I start yelling. Soon, the owner of the boat yells back for our address, tells us the boat is full, but he'll be back. It's John and Connie, our neighbors up the street, taking everyone they can to higher ground.

I climb down the attic stairs, wade past floating furniture, unlock and open the front door to see blue skies, a bright sunny day and eight feet of water. I wade back to the attic to get our things together in a large garbage bag to keep them dry. I finally catch the cat and stuff him into a pillowcase despite his howling protest. After several hours, the boat returns almost full again, but with just enough room for Lynn and me, two dogs, a cat and a bird in a cage.

John pulls the boat up to the porch, helps us all in, and we shove off for higher ground about one mile away. The streets are difficult to navigate because of all the submerged vehicles, downed powerlines and uprooted trees blocking our path, but we finally arrive at Mike's Hardware on Elysian Fields Avenue, about a block from Gentilly Boulevard. We unload the boat and wade up to Mike's and the only dry land we can see for blocks around.

Mr. Mike was staying in his store to protect it from looters. After about 40 of us gather around his store, he unlocks the door so we can use his toilet and brings out a generator for lights and a fan. Everyone is pulling together like one big family to take care of each other. We share what little food and water we have; even the dog food is shared so our pets won't be hungry. The sun has set, it's starting to get dark, and it's time to arrange our few clothes to make a bed on the ground next to the building. As I fall asleep, I think how lucky we are that we are not trapped in our attic, and we have our pets with us. It could be a lot worse.

Wednesday 8.31.05

We wake up to another quiet, sunny day. Someone has a flatboat and a couple of guys take it up the street a few blocks to Rite-Aid and Walgreen drug stores to get food, water and medicine. The glass doors are already smashed by looters taking radios and DVD players and other useless things, while we are looking to keep body and soul together. Mary, the nurse in our group, dispenses the medicine to the sick among us, and rations the food and water so that everyone has some.

The temperature is starting to rise and so is the smell from the polluted water, so only one more trip for water is made with the flatboat. Next to the hardware store is a drive-through bank which provides shelter from the sun. The water has receded enough so that there are islands between the flooded car lanes where we can camp out until the sun sets.

Several times during the afternoon Coast Guard boats come from Franklin Avenue and I–610 to take people back up to the interstate for possible bus rides to the Superdome for evacuation. I can't say why, but there are few takers. Perhaps we feel safe where we are, even though we're running out of food and water and can't stay very much longer.

Other boats come by taking the very sick to the University of New Orleans campus and then to the Lakefront Airport nearby. Soon after, a guy named Brian comes wading up the street from I-610 where he and others had just spent the last 21 hours in the sun all day with no food, water or shade waiting for buses that never came.

We swap stories and share some soup, then sack out on our little islands for one more night. With all the lights out in the city, the sky is full of more stars than I have ever seen, with the moon in conjunction with Jupiter and Venus setting in the west.

Thursday 9.1.05

Today something has to give. We can't stay here and run out of food and water. We're not sure where we should go or how to get there. The chemistry of the group changes when another group of about ten people shows up bearing armfuls of clothing and backpacks with the tags still on them and bottles of alcohol and beer. They're unwilling to share the food and water they have, but they line up to eat and drink what little we have left. Mike explains to them how this survival thing works; they nod and seem to understand but continue to be apart, hoarding their supplies and getting drunk.

After a few tense hours, they finally leave, and we get back to figuring out our next move.

Suddenly, it starts to rain. Mike brings out some tarps from his hardware store to make a shelter for a propane stove while we peel shrimp, onion, potato and garlic gathered from freezers in the neighborhood to make our last meal here. Others are catching rainwater from the downspouts to fill water bottles and wash ourselves. The dogs will drink water only from our cupped hands, the cat not at all. We try forcing capfuls down his throat to no avail. Sammy has taken no food or water since we left the attic Tuesday afternoon.

Around 5:00 p.m., we hear helicopters landing in the football field behind the store. I put the cat into a discarded backpack, grab the dogs and the birdcage and the bag with the rest of our stuff, and we hustle over to the field. Ten of us, along with the animals, are loaded into the helicopter, which takes off immediately, banking sharply to reveal the massive flooding in our neighborhood and surrounding area. Lynn puts her arms around a couple of older women and tries to calm them. Neither has ever flown before, and this first time is a memorable one. The trip is noisy, exciting and too short. After only a few minutes we set down on a runway at the New Orleans Lakefront Airport.

We haul everything out of the helicopter and head for another runway about 100 yards away. There we get in a long line of people waiting to be airlifted to somewhere else. Rumors are flying about where that might be. Some say Baton Rouge. Some say Houston. Nobody knows anything for sure. There are about 400 people in line ahead of us, and, since we arrived a few hours ago, another thousand have joined the queue. Coast Guard helicopters continue all night to bring in more people, bottled water and food, making it impossible to sleep. The wash from the propellers sandblasts everyone on the tarmac, blowing food boxes, water bottles and assorted trash as far as the eye can see. The night drags on. More people continue to arrive and line up under the glare of huge bright light from an airport emergency disaster fire truck. There is exactly one portable toilet for everyone to use and it looks as if everyone has used it. It is full to overflowing and there is a line of fifty people waiting to use it. Soon a handful of state troopers arrive to try to keep some semblance of order in a line of people constantly shifting and moving around. At long last the sun starts to rise on a new day of uncertainty and waiting.

Friday 9.2.05

At 10:00 a.m., the line starts to surge forward. There is much grumbling about people cutting into line ahead of them, and the troopers are yelling for everyone to quit pushing and shoving. A man we knew from Mike's Hardware doesn't listen when troopers tell him to get back in line. After another warning, the trooper shoots him with a taser. When they zap him a second time, they have his full attention, and he starts moving towards the back of the line.

The line begins to move forward again in fits and starts, and after two hours it's our turn. We make a mad dash across the runway with two dogs, a cat, and a bird to board a Chinook helicopter that has about 40 people in it. We are flown to the other side of town and dropped off at Armstrong International Airport. There the real fun begins.

We are directed to the stairs that go up to the main lobby where we see thousands of people going in all directions. Some are standing in lines that snake around the lobby without knowing what to expect at the end. Federal Police are everywhere, but they have no answers to any questions. They are there for crowd control until planes come to fly all the people out. We find a space against the wall out of the way of most of the crowd and settle in for a long wait.

We watch as emergency medical teams run here and there tending to people having heart attacks and other problems. Since there is no chance of getting any sleep, I take the dogs on their leashes to look for a place to walk them. We go outside onto the elevated ramp and find nothing but concrete. The dogs are too nervous to do anything, and they haven't eaten in two days. The ramp is lined with FEMA trucks, emergency vehicles, and evacuees who seem to be living on the ramp, in no hurry to leave. We head back inside the terminal. I leave the animals with Lynn while I look for a payphone that might work. What I discover is that the entire 504 area code is down, and there is no way to get word out that we are OK. I go back to sit with

Lynn and wait, try to sleep, wait some more while the hours crawl by.

Finally, the police use bullhorns to announce that everyone should start lining up to get on planes that will take us out of this swamp. We continue to sit on the sidelines. The line is impossibly long and doesn't move for hours. We would rather sit where we are and wait for things to clear out than stand in line where people are falling out due to heat, exhaustion and lack of medication.

The police are yelling through bullhorns to give up all pens, lighters, nail clippers, guns, and knives and throw them into garbage cans being held aloft. Almost everyone seems to have something to throw, and the cans fill quickly. There is more pushing and shoving, medics being called, as people fight to get in line to wait. As we sit across the terminal from all the commotion, we see a relatively short line that seems to be for those with medical problems. Some are using walkers and canes; some are in wheelchairs or on stretchers.

It is now about 2:30 a.m. Saturday morning. I have a strong urge to make a move, and it has to be now. We gather up the pets and our bag of stuff and get into the short line. No one tries to stop us, and we just keep moving. An hour and a half later, we reach the security checkpoint where the TSA people check us out and let us go through with no problem. We go down the steps and across the runway to where an Army C130 transport plane is loading people for takeoff. We go up a ramp in the rear of this huge plane and are told to wait until the front of the plane fills up, so we will be in the rear with all the pets around us.

The floor of the plane fills with 150 people sitting shoulder to shoulder. We sit in the last row with the two dogs in our laps, the birdcage to my back, and the cat in the backpack, which I wear on my chest. Another TV crew turns their camera on us, sticks a mic in our faces, and marvels that we all managed to get out together. As if we had a choice.

It's been almost five days since Katrina blew through, taking our old lives with her. As the sun starts to rise, I get one last glimpse of my town as the engines rev up and the ramp slowly closes. Conflicting emotions well up inside: sadness that we have to leave, joy to be getting away from all the craziness. Once everyone is strapped in, we all want to know where we are heading. The crew says they're not sure. They tell us it could be Houston or San Antonio, maybe Atlanta. Finally, the captain informs us that we are on our way to Austin, as Houston and San Antonio are already full. Atlanta would have been all right, as our daughter and her family live there and would put us up until things get settled. But it's Austin, and I don't really mind. I've heard lots of good things about Austin, and I'm looking forward to going someplace I've never been. The flight takes less than two hours, and we land just outside Austin at a military air base.

Saturday 9.3.05

When we land, we find rows of city buses lined up to take us to a shelter. When the bus we get on is full, a man steps on to tell us that there are snacks and drinks for us in the front, and we'll be leaving soon. As we leave the airport, I start to feel giddy, mostly from lack of sleep, but also from the view of an alien yet familiar landscape I see through the window. It's been thirty years since I was in Texas, and I had forgotten how really big the sky is. The bus ride takes half an hour, and we pull into the rear of the Austin Convention Center in downtown Austin.

From the moment I step off the bus I feel as though I have entered a parallel universe. Every step we take is guided by caring, concerned volunteers who seem to want nothing but to make us as comfortable as possible. The building is crawling with them. When I look around as if I might need help or information, someone is there asking what they can do to help me find what I need.

After getting off the bus, we walk up a ramp into the center to a medical triage set up to care for those with immediate medical needs. We fill out forms and talk to EMS volunteers from the police and fire departments. Our medical histories are noted along with any prescription drugs we are taking and may need. From there, we are taken to the other side of the center, where we are processed by volunteers at computers and given orange wristbands to wear to show that we belong there. The wristband also allows us to come and go as we please. Our personal information is put into the computer, so people who may be looking for us can find us. Air mattresses are being inflated and bedding distributed, so we have a place to steep.

Finally, we are handed over to people from the Austin Humane Society, who take our pets to be cared for at the animal shelter. After talking to these wonderful volunteers, we know that our pets are in good hands, and, for the first time in a week, we can quit worrying about them. They are not in the best of shape, but we know they soon will be. I think the whole ordeal was harder on them than us, but we all got out alive and together.

Now that the burden of constantly caring for the pets has been lifted, we are free to look after our own needs. In the next section of the building, breakfast is being served. There are too many items in the food line to list them all, but it is all hot and fresh and it was the best we had eaten in a week. Full and content, we make our way back to our bed, which, though only a couple of inches thick, feels like a feather bed compared to the concrete and asphalt we had been sleeping on. I fall into a deep sleep, oblivious to the bright overhead lights and the general murmur of the crowd of people all around. While I'm sleeping like the dead, a woman from the *Wall Street Journal* interviews Lynn about the ordeal of getting out of New Orleans with all of our animals. She had heard about us from the people at the Humane Society where she was doing a story about the pets of evacuees. She came to the center and managed to find us. The story will run in three days.

When I finally wake up, I go to search for some clothes to replace the ones we've been wearing since we left our house. The Red Cross volunteers have set up tables full to overflowing with everything we need to start a new wardrobe, including items for personal hygiene. When I get back, I see more and more beds are being added as more people start to flood in. Before it is over, there will be 4,200 souls in the center, many of them children who seem to view their situation as a great adventure.

While we are lying around in bed wondering what will happen next, two young volunteers come down the aisle carrying a cell phone. They tell us a woman is on the phone who wants to help out by sharing her three-bedroom home with an older, "mature," couple. Lynn is 60, and I'm 56, so I guess we qualify. My first impulse is to say no. We don't know this person; she doesn't know us. But if she is willing to take a blind chance on us, how can we refuse her generosity? I take the phone and tell her, yes, we would be honored to accept her kind offer, but we're still kind of goofy from lack of sleep, and could she pick us up the next morning. She agrees, and we pass out again, waking up in time for dinner. After another delicious meal, we wander around the center watching the enormous rooms fill up with more beds and more evacuees. I know I am one of them, but at the same time I feel apart because Lynn and I have been touched by the kindness of an angel. All over the center, large screen projection TV's have been set up showing Katrina news 24/7. I am horrified by what I see on the screen yet unable to look away.

As I watch, I see my beautiful city being destroyed first by the floodwaters and then by violent, lawless people. I am too emotionally fragile to continue watching and have to tear myself away from the madness I see on the screen. As I look around me at what is happening in the shelter, I realize that the whole world is not going crazy. The wonderful folks in Austin are doing everything possible to create a safe haven for us, and for right now that is enough.

As I make my way back to our bed, I talk to people and listen to their stories. I find out what part of town they lived in, how high the water rose in their homes, and how they made it to this place. I hear no complaints, no whining, only gratitude that they made it here alive, and hope for a better tomorrow. As I crawl into bed, which is soft and dry, wearing clothes that are clean and dry, I say a prayer for those who have not yet escaped the ravaged city.

Sunday 9.4.05

As I slowly wake up to a new day, I have the feeling that time has stopped. There are no windows to the outside world and the overhead lights are always on. I only want to stay in this little cocoon we have spun for ourselves. There is nowhere we have to be, nothing we have to do, and it's tempting to just lie here and let the world go by, but we have a date with an angel. And besides, I'm starving. After a quick breakfast we pack up our things, feeling grateful we don't have to worry about the animals. We miss them terribly, but now they are in good hands. At the appointed time, we leave the shelter to wait on the curb for our ride.

We don't have to wait long. Our angel arrives, and her name is Kristen. She helps us load our things into her SUV, and off we go. As we head west out of Austin to a town called Dripping Springs, she tells us that her refrigerator and pantry are full and not to ask for anything, just take whatever we want. About twenty minutes later, we arrive at her three-bedroom, two-bath house that sits on two acres at the beginning of the foothills. Her husband, James, and their brown Labrador Retriever, Tex, come out to meet us as we pull into the driveway. On the way to the house, I have the strange feeling of coming home to a place I've never been. This feeling is accompanied by the weird sensation of time stopping again. Suddenly, there is all the time in the world to do nothing at all, or just sit on the porch in the evening and watch the deer grazing in the yard. Hours seem to stretch to infinity, and a calm descends that is very healing to the soul.

It's quiet out here in the country and very dark at night, two things I missed living in a city that rarely sleeps. There is time enough now to reflect on how blessed we have been, how generous people have been with their time and effort and their checkbooks. Being here gives me a chance to reconnect with the far-flung members of my family, some of whom I haven't talked to in years. After assuring everyone that we are safe and mostly sound, we spend the rest of the day Sunday just sitting around talking quietly or not at all and munching on sandwiches and chips when we are hungry. Kristen and James are the perfect hosts. They seem to know when to leave us alone while quietly making sure we have everything we need. They both rise early for work, so it's early to bed. We retire to our own room to fall into a real feather bed that makes us feel like we're floating on a cloud. There are no lights, no sound, and soon the world disappears.

Monday 9.5.05

It's been one week since Lynn and I crawled into our attic with our pets to escape the rising water in New Orleans. Now sitting here in the home of Kristen and James, it almost seems like a bad dream. Every minute Kirsten isn't working, she's driving us around to buy us things we need, taking us back to the shelter to get prescriptions filled, helping us get financial assistance, and going online to get useful information.

Meanwhile, in Atlanta, our daughter, Connie, and her husband, Doug, are doing all they can to line up an apartment for us and housing assistance so we'll have a place in which to start over.

There are so many family, friends, and strangers to thank for what we have. It's difficult to know where to begin, but it was surely providence that guided our steps and protected us, two dogs, a cat, and a bird.

Afterword: Breaches of Faith

Fredrick Barton

For the last 29 years Fredrick Barton has worked as an English professor at the University of New Orleans, and for 22 of those years, he has held positions in the UNO administration. From 2003 to the present, he has served as Provost and Vice Chancellor for Academic and Student Affairs. He was among those administrators who sequestered themselves in a small room of a building on a sister school's campus in order to resurrect The University of New Orleans, whose campus was decimated, and whose entire population was evacuated and unable to communicate with one another.

The premise of the Katrina Narrative Project began with the notion that everyone has a story and that a comprehensive understanding of any disastrous event can only be achieved by knowing the individual experiences of those affected by the catastrophe. This book arises from the efforts of University of New Orleans students and faculty to capture and preserve the stories of the affected.

Katrina's winds died away in a matter of hours, and its flood waters were pumped out in a few weeks, but the long aftermath of its devastation continues to the day of this writing in November of 2007 and will continue for years longer into the future. The only appropriate analogy for what happened here is that of war. Imagine that New Orleans was hit by a nuclear bomb. Two years and more after the storm, only about half of our residents have returned to our city, not exclusively because only about half of our housing stock has been returned to habitability. Some 1,100 of our fellow citizens died, and a quarter million remain displaced, many now, no doubt permanently. But among those who survived, all were displaced for at least a month while the city was drained, the burst levees temporarily patched and the basic elements of city services—water, gas and electricity—placed at least intermittently, and in restricted locations, back on line.

The national media have portrayed the destruction of New Orleans as an African-American story. And since prior to Katrina 72% of our citizens in the municipality of New Orleans were black, and since our black citizens were more likely to be poor, documented suffering in the African-American community has been established as vast and profound. Nonetheless, Katrina was a color-blind and class-indifferent scourge, and the torments of her flood waters were inflicted on New Orleanians of every skin pigment and income bracket. The houses in the storied Lower 9th Ward, where most of the residents were working-class African-Americans, were washed off their foundations. But the damage was just as extensive in New Orleans East where most of the residents were middle- and professional-class African Americans. And the flooding was even deeper in Lakeview where most of the residents were middle-class whites. And lest we forget, though the flooding was the worst in Orleans Parish, plenty of people in the predominantly white suburban Jefferson, Plaquemines and St. Bernard parishes suffered devastating flooding as well.

There can be no doubt that, as is always true, recovery has been easier for the more prosperous of our citizens. Those with adequate insurance have been able to rebuild more quickly than those who have had to rely on federal emergency funding that has been administered in the state bureaucratic Purgatory called The Road Home Program. But whether we managed to resume residence in the city by mid-October of 2005, as perhaps some 75,000 were able, or whether we still live in Atlanta or Houston, those regarding themselves New Orleanians still greet each other upon a first post-Katrina meeting by asking, "How did you do in the storm?" That's because we all know that we all suffered to a greater or lesser degree. The unluckiest among us lost their lives or the lives of loved ones; perhaps half our citizens escaped with their lives and little more; most everyone suffered loss of possessions and life's mementoes along with expensive, inconvenient and time-consuming damage to their homes. Even those who lived in the "sliver by the river," the ribbon of land along the

Mississippi that did not flood, suffered loss of access to their homes for weeks and sundry economic setbacks.

Thus Katrina was an ironically democratizing force. History divided on August 29, 2005, into two distinctly different periods: before the storm, and after the storm. "Katrina" itself was a name unnecessarily and infrequently invoked as people spoke of their experiences in "the storm." The wrenching details vary from individual to individual, but each New Orleanian knows that no other New Orleanian escaped untouched and consequently unchanged by this unprecedented and psychologically debilitating event. "How did you do in the storm?" proceeds from an understanding, however painful, of something shared.

Everyone has a story. And with regard to Katrina, this is mine.

Though no major storm made a direct hit on New Orleans between Hurricane Betsy in 1965 and Hurricane Katrina in 2005, hurricane tracking is a summer ritual for large numbers of the city's residents. *The Times-Picayune* publishes an annual storm guide early each summer with suggestions about supplies to acquire and evacuation routes to contemplate. The local television weather broadcasts chart the progress of tropical disturbances from the time they whirl into life off the west coast of Africa until they blow themselves out days and even weeks later. And particularly since about 1990, environmental reporting by Mark Schleifstein and others has made New Orleanians increasingly aware of our escalating vulnerability. Global warming has led to more, and more intense, storms. And the combination of rising sea levels and the disappearance of coastal wetlands (a phenomenon the product of both climate change and direct human activities: oil and gas exploration, ship-canal building and lower Mississippi River flood control projects) has brought New Orleans closer to open water and a storm's undiminished wrath. Moreover, warnings by Schleifstein and his colleagues in the engineering and scientific communities have alerted us to the scenarios by which a powerful storm could push enough water into Lake Pontchartrain to top its levees and flood most of the city behind the levees' protection.

Yet, even as late as 1992, even in the face of a storm as deadly as Category 4 Hurricane Andrew, which passed just south of the city, few New Orleanians evacuated. More of our citizens took refuge outside the city when Category 2 Hurricane Georges threatened us in 1998 before curling east to make landfall near the Mississippi/Alabama border. But though my wife Joyce and I contemplated joining the evacuees in 1998, we ultimately stayed in our Uptown New Orleans house. We remained at home through the aggravation of nearly three days without electricity largely because we had no history of leaving. Our families had remained in their homes through the storms of our childhoods in the 1950s, through the direct hit of Betsy in 1965 and the near miss of Camille in 1969. So we stayed through Andrew and through Georges, too, although we were so uncomfortable without air conditioning in the searing aftermath of the 1998 storm we castigated ourselves for not having left for that reason alone.

Joyce and I did finally evacuate for Category 4 Hurricane Ivan in 2004, and most of the city went with us. The evacuation was a harrowing mess. People reported exhausting trips taking 17 hours and longer to drive from New Orleans to Houston, a destination normally only five hours away. Inching along Interstate 10 at speeds around ten miles per hour, Joyce and I took eight hours, instead of the usual hour and 15 minutes, to reach a motel on the eastern side of Baton Rouge, the only hotel accommodations we were able to secure anywhere within 300 miles of New Orleans. Then, following a path similar to that of Georges, Ivan twisted off to the east at the last minute and did very little damage in New Orleans. Joyce and I returned to our home only 36 hours after fleeing for Ivan. We arrived back in the city thinking we'd learned something, swearing we'd never fight that evacuation traffic again. This, we later discovered, was Ivan's evil anti-lesson, and our mastering it would cost us.

I first became aware of Katrina on Wednesday, August 24, 2005. At that time it was a Category 1 storm in the Atlantic predicted to make landfall somewhere on the American East Coast. I gave it little thought. By the morning of Friday, August 26, however, Katrina had cut across the Florida peninsula and entered the Gulf of Mexico. Its computer projections were tracking significantly westward, though still far east of us. The westward movement lasted throughout the day, and at 4:30 on that last day of our first week of school that fall, several administrators, including UNO Chancellor Tim Ryan, gathered in my office for a conversation about the storm. If Katrina went ashore as it was then projected, it would strike several hundred miles to our east, leaving us well out of harm's way. Nonetheless, we all agreed to watch the storm overnight and, if necessary, meet about it on campus at noon the next day. Already late, we then adjourned to attend a beginning-of-the-year cocktail party for faculty and staff in the University Center across the street from the Administration Building.

The cocktail party ran until about 7 p.m. amid much discussion of the storm. I vividly recall telling two new faculty members with young children that if I were in their circumstances and had somewhere I could go for the weekend, I would take off the first thing in the morning. Even as I offered this advice, however, I chided myself a bit for being so overly cautious. The storm was not going to affect us. And I knew that I wouldn't have taken such advice myself, even if my university duties had allowed it.

After the faculty/staff party, I wandered out to the New Student Luau, which was just getting underway in the quad between the University Center and the Recreation and Fitness Center. Our student activities coordinators had arranged good food and music for our students, and the new enrollees were out in impressive numbers. We had just instituted significantly higher enrollment standards, but our enrollment had not declined as we had feared. As always, our students arrived in a delightfully diverse mix. Over a quarter of our students were African-American and nearly half qualified as minority. About ten percent were international students from almost 100 different countries. And all this wonderful rainbow of young humanity seemed to have turned out for the luau that night. So it was with bursting pride and considerable pleasure that I milled about that evening greeting the new students and congratulating staffers Pam Rault and Roberto Diaz del Valle on a job well done. A good breeze was blowing, making the New Orleans summer night unseasonably comfortable, and I lingered longer than I might have otherwise. UNO seemed headed in a promising direction, poised to realize our considerable dreams for it as an educational leader for our entire region. That night, with an energized enrollment of 17,250, is a place to which, two years after the storm, we long to return.

Upon arriving home for dinner just after eight that night of August 26, Joyce warned me that Katrina's computer projections had shifted still again. The storm was intensifying, and it threatened to go ashore on the Mississippi Gulf Coast, only about 100 miles to the east. As we ate that night, Joyce and I talked about the now looming possible need to evacuate. But rather than fear ruling our discussion, as it no doubt should have, exasperation dominated our exchanges. The prospect of being stalled again on I-10 was aggravating, and we weren't even on the road yet. We went to bed with the stubborn hope that the storm would stay to our east and weaken and that we wouldn't have to run.

But, of course, no such luck. Joyce was up on Saturday the 27th and on the computer by five a.m.; the news was wretched. Projections now had Katrina making a direct hit on our city as a Category 5 storm. I began to make preparations to leave while waiting until seven to call Chancellor Ryan to arrange for an earlier meeting of the UNO administrative group. We met on campus at nine and activated our hurricane emergency plan, each of us in the meeting contacting our unit supervisors to inform them that we were closing campus, securing our buildings, arranging for the buses to evacuate those of our students without their own transportation and, to protect it from damage, shutting down our conventional Internet and e-mail operations by the end of the day. As I rang off with each of the deans and directors who reported to me, I wished them safety and told them that I would see them soon, presumably on Tuesday, the day after the storm would pass. We all commented that we hoped we could resume classes on Wednesday and that way lose only one day in each class sequence. Ultimately, we would lose the entire beginning of the semester, of course, and would have to start over with a new, reworked array of classes seven weeks later.

By the time I got back to my Uptown house around 2:30, Joyce had what then seemed encouraging news. She had managed to find us airline tickets on a flight out of town that night. We had joked in the early morning that we would be happy to book "tickets to anywhere," just to avoid the inevitable traffic snarl, but Joyce had bought tickets on a 7 p.m. Delta flight to Raleigh-Durham, North Carolina, less than an hour's drive from Sanford where my mother lived. Our dual middle-class incomes would enable us to execute this evacuation with minimal inconvenience. Weren't we smart!

The year before, for Ivan, we had packed our car with all kinds of supplies, had remembered to pack financial records and grab a bag of treasured photographs. We also packed a week's worth of clothes and such nicer items of clothing as business suits for each of us. Looking back, I think we took Ivan more seriously and made better preparations for what might have been a longer evacuation. But Ivan was a hurricane season's example of "cry wolf," and our experience with Ivan focused on our annoyed inconvenience, thereby diluting our appropriate fear. We'd be home on Tuesday, we presumed, so we took only four days' change of underwear. With no business to do, we packed only jeans, shorts and T-shirts. We took a checkbook and ATM cards, but none of the financial records we had carefully packed out the year before. Our major worry at the time focused on getting to the airport. The Ivan evacuation route to Baton Rouge ran right past the airport, and it had taken us three hours to reach that point. If we were going to reach the airport with an hour's lead time before our flight, we needed to leave only 30 minutes after I'd gotten home from the university.

Then a new problem arose. We called airport parking to make sure we could store our car and were told that, though there were spaces available now, they were "filling up fast." So we changed plans and ordered a cab. I parked my car, the nicest car I'd ever owned and only a year old, in our garage next to Joyce's Mustang convertible, a surprise birthday gift from me two years earlier. We would never drive these cars again.

But our concern at the time was that our taxi didn't arrive as scheduled at 3:15 and had still not arrived 30 minutes later. It was now almost certainly too late to find an airport parking spot. Were we going to have to drive out after all? And if so, where were we going to stay? Because we had airline reservations, clever us, we hadn't tried to book a motel room, and the closest room available might now be north of Memphis. In an atmosphere of suppressed panic, we called another cab company and were fortunately picked up shortly after four.

The traffic along Earhart Expressway and Airline Highway was exactly as we feared, and Joyce and I worried our watches as we crept along; the drive that normally takes twenty minutes, lasted two and a half hours. Along the way, we talked with our driver, a thin African-American man in a snap-brim cap who appeared to be in his late sixties or early seventies. A hint of gray whiskers suggested he'd been working since early morning, but his pressed white shirt remained crisp. What was he going to do for the storm, we inquired. He'd probably just stay home, he told us. We were his last fare of the day, and after that, he'd park his cab, which he didn't own, in a raised lot. His own car was in pretty good condition, a nice big Oldsmobile, he said, though it leaked a bit of oil. He'd driven it out for Ivan in a caravan with his brother, their mother, and their two families. They drove all the way past Jackson, Mississippi, up Interstate 55 but couldn't find a single place to stay. Ended up having to sleep in their cars, and he wasn't going to do that again. Anyway, the weathermen always seemed to get it wrong because the storms never came to New Orleans. We told him we thought he ought to watch the news carefully and consider getting out, but he said he probably wouldn't leave this time under much of any circumstances. As he dropped us at the airport less than 30 minutes before our scheduled flight, we wondered if he would turn out to be the smart one. Just avoid the aggravation, go home and wait for Katrina to turn east as had so many other storms before. I think of that cab driver often, always with a prayer that he changed his mind and got himself and his family to safety.

One might imagine that Louis Armstrong airport was a madhouse, but it was more like a vast cathedral at twilight. The cafes and shops were closed. The unused gate lounges hunkered in darkness. As if a plane might leave before its departure time, no one milled about. And in those gate areas still operating, people spoke to each other in whispers. Joyce and I were on a 70-seat plane departing from Gate 2. The rest of the Delta concourse was dark. A nervous woman in her late forties sat down beside me. She was dressed in a pink suit and red shoes, and she looked tired. She wanted to know if I thought she might be able to stand by for our flight to Raleigh-Durham. I told her I had no idea. She said she was from Chicago but just wanted to leave, just wanted to go anywhere away from this storm. She was in town for a convention and was supposed to go home the next day, but she had heard rumors the airport was shutting down and wouldn't support any flights out on Sunday. She mentioned that she had flown into New Orleans on American, and I told her I suspected she'd be more likely to get standby privileges on her ticketed airline than on another one. But American had told her their planes were full and had suggested she try other carriers. A few moments after she spoke with me, I saw her talking with the Delta gate agent and then slowly walking back toward the main terminal. I doubt she found an empty seat that night, and, like the cab driver, I have worried about her ever since. She would have had a hard time finding transportation back to her hotel in downtown New Orleans, and she actually wouldn't have wanted to end up there anyway. I can only assume that the next several days were among the worst in her life.

Many have wondered why the airlines ended operations out of New Orleans on Saturday night when planes could have landed and departed from New Orleans until late Sunday afternoon at the earliest. Couldn't a superior hurricane evacuation plan have brought in more, rather than the usual number of, planes and gotten more people to safety? Yes, of course. But that would have required America, the State of Louisiana and the people of Greater New Orleans to have understood the disaster that was now less than 36 hours away. Under the direction of no one but their profit-focused executives, the airlines were involved in no one's evacuation plans. They were also, no doubt, acutely aware of staff shrinkage. All their New-Orleans-based employees had their own evacuation and that of their families to worry about. The airlines might have been able to get pilots, flight attendants and planes into Armstrong. But could they count on ground personnel to show up for work? In sufficient and reliable numbers, probably not. So Saturday night was the end of air travel, and Joyce and I were on the last plane out of Dodge. If, for whatever reason, it didn't fly, we were in the same circumstances as the distraught lady in the pink suit, in our case about 12 miles from home and no way to get there. You can imagine our discomfort when the departure was delayed.

About a half hour after we were supposed to have lifted off and about an hour after we were supposed to have boarded, two uniformed Delta agents walked by, and I overheard one of them say that the plane was overbooked. Somebody who was sitting in the departure lounge had a ticket but no seat. Maybe several somebodies. Maybe me and Joyce.

Finally, the boarding process commenced, and Joyce and I were able to settle into our seats near the back of the 70-seat Embraer with its single-seat row down the left-hand side and two-abreast seats down the right. Whoever was the victim of the overbooking must have been notified and dealt with in the lounge because no dispute over seats broke out among the people who were allowed aboard. But a long delay followed after all the passengers were seat-belted in, and Joyce and I exchanged our continuing concerns that the flight might yet be cancelled. Finally, a gate agent, a flight attendant and a pilot stood together in the front of the plane to announce that the aircraft was overweight and that they needed four passengers to deplane. When no one volunteered, they offered enticements: hotel rooms in the downtown Hilton and two-hundred-dollar flight coupons. No one raised a hand, so they upped the ante to include four-hundred-dollar flight coupons. Still, no one agreed to surrender a seat.

I whispered to Joyce, "They aren't going to get anyone off this plane without a police escort."

She said, "Fluff your jacket up around you and start looking skinny."

Delta's effort to get four people off our plane remains a mystery to me. If we were really overweight, they must have solved the problem by pulling off luggage, for no passenger deplaned. A few minutes later we pushed back from the gate and taxied away from an almost dark airport. Joyce and I held hands as we roared west down the runway, still spooked by the overweight announcement. Others, we learned, tamped down the same fear, and after the plane lifted off and seemed to gain critical altitude, relieved applause broke out throughout the passenger cabin. Out over the wetlands of the Bonnet Carre Spillway, the plane banked right and flew in a rising arc over Interstate 10 where cars with their headlights pointing west seemed to be parked for miles in either direction.

From the refuge of my mother's house in North Carolina, along with the rest of America, Joyce and I watched on television as Hurricane Katrina slammed ashore. At the last minute, the storm made the slightest jog to the east, an incomplete twist of the sort that had spared our city from the ravages of Georges and Ivan. The winds also lessened before the storm reached New Orleans, falling from Category 5 to Category 3 (subsequent analyses have suggested they may have slowed even more than that). The city took the shock wave of wind and largely held. The levees, raised in the 1980s, proved high enough and were not overtopped. National news reporters assayed the damage and announced more than once that, "New Orleans has dodged a bullet," and moved on to provide storm reports from Gulfport, Mississippi, and Mobile, Alabama. That was the standard message across the television dial. New Orleans had dodged a bullet, we were told, and Joyce and I went to sleep in my mother's guest bedroom in Sanford, North Carolina, on August 29, 2005, with prayers of thanksgiving for our city's salvation.

But as we held each other in exhausted relief, the worst was happening. The levees had, in fact, breached hours earlier. The poorly constructed, inadequately maintained levees were high enough but not strong enough, and they burst from the pressure of the high water behind them. We had been schooled to fear a storm surge great enough to dump water over the top of our levees into the bowl of our city. But no one had ever warned us they could simply fail, and they did in at least six places: one on the 17th Street Canal, two on the London Avenue Canal, and three on the Industrial Canal. And seemingly, none of this was understood in its entirety for days.

Tuesday, August 30, 2005, started off with good news that proved entirely misleading. We woke to a phone call from our neighbor Don Tyler who looks after our house when we're out of town. Don had evacuated to Galveston, Texas, but had taken contact numbers with him. And just minutes earlier he had spoken with another neighbor who had stayed in the city. Our houses were fine. There were some roof tiles in the yards, and lots of tree debris. But there were no broken windows, and none of the giant oaks that shade our homes had fallen.

Our conversation with Don marked the high point of our post-storm optimism. Within the hour, we were startled when TV news began to report the breach on the 17th Street Canal. Joyce and I knew instantly the horror this meant, and we didn't know a fifth of what was really going on because no one seemed to have discovered that other levees had failed as well. For a time we clung to a desperate hope that plans to drop railroad boxcars into the 17th Street Canal breach would plug the hole and stop the flood. But as that day wore on and gave way to the nightmarish blur of the days to come, officials announced that they had no recourse but to let the lake "equalize" inside the bowl of the city. New Orleanians, wherever they had fled, watched as their city filled with water. Soon, the airwaves burst with footage of terrified people being plucked from rooftops in baskets lowered from Coast Guard helicopters. And then came the wrenching reports of the suffering of people abandoned in the Superdome and the Convention Center. Buses didn't arrive to transport them to safety. A vicious heat wave added to their misery. Ultimately, outrage and anger flared. And, inevitably, some violence, too. But much of what the broadcast media reported was exaggerated. No one was beheaded. No children were raped. But there's little question that in the withering heat of the days after Katrina, New Orleans went to hell.

Among the many lessons that Katrina taught the modern Americans of Greater New Orleans was that technology is frail and exceedingly unreliable in times of crisis. In the days during the evacuation and those immediately afterwards, cell phones didn't work, presumably because everybody's trying to use them at once overloaded all working circuits. And the storm fog was exacerbated by the haste in which everyone necessarily fled. Joyce and I didn't know where our friends, neighbors and professional colleagues were located, and we couldn't reach them on cell phones that didn't work. In what now seems almost improbable foresight, UNO Chancellor Tim Ryan and I had exchanged the land-line phone numbers of the family members offering us refuge, and so we were able to stay in contact. Eventually, we both discovered that text messaging on our cell phones still functioned, as did many other adults who had never used text messaging before, and with that understanding we were gradually able to make contact with our vice chancellors and deans. By Wednesday evening we decided that, as soon as possible, our team of senior administrators should gather in Baton Rouge to devise and implement a recovery plan for our university.

The primary problem with the plan to headquarter in Baton Rouge was housing. Louisiana's capital city, only 80 miles from New Orleans, had suffered very little hurricane damage. But it was now chock full of evacuees. All hotel rooms were full for hundreds of miles around the city. New Orleanians were crowded into the homes of Baton Rouge family members and friends. Our Vice Chancellor for Campus Services, Joel Chatelain, stayed along with 10 family members in a 1,500-square-foot, two-bedroom, one-bathroom house owned by his wife's aunt. Our Dean of Engineering, Russ Trahan, crowded into the house of his wife's aunt in Erwinville, Louisiana, about 20 miles from Baton Rouge, with 18 people sharing her home's two bathrooms. Our Associate Vice Chancellor for Institutional Effectiveness, Scott Whittenburg, could find housing no closer than St. Martinville, an hour-and-15-minute commute away, where he and his two children slept on air mattresses and a couch in the home of a family Scott had met only casually on just a handful of occasions.

UNO Chancellor Tim Ryan had evacuated to Georgia by car, and he returned to Louisiana on Thursday, September 1, 2005. LSU System officials arranged a room for him first at the Faculty Club and within a week had found an apartment for him at their Pennington Research Center. But even though he was a senior state executive trying to take charge of an historic crisis, they did not provide these accommodations for him free of charge or even at a reduced rate. Still, he was grateful for a place to lay his head so that he could get to work. In the days immediately after the storm, system officials made no comparable arrangements for UNO's other top administrators. We were completely on our own.

I needed to get to Baton Rouge as soon as possible, but given that Joyce and I had flown out of New Orleans, getting back to the area was no easy matter. The New Orleans airport was shut down and being used as an emergency medical facility. There were a limited number of flights into Baton Rouge, but I was at a loss for ground transportation if I flew in. Internet research revealed there were no cars to rent or buy within several hundred miles of Baton Rouge. The wisest course seemed the purchase of an automobile in North Carolina to drive back to Louisiana.

We found a used car to buy in Fayetteville, about an hour south of my mother's. Heawatha "Pete" Sanders at the Fayetteville CarMax showed us great kindness. He was quite concerned, however, when I explained that I wanted to write a check on a bank located in New Orleans, which was now under water, and I wanted to drive the car away that very day. Normally, a car dealership deals with a local bank, or, in the case of an out-of-state bank, holds the car until the check clears. I didn't have the time to open an account in North Carolina, and I didn't have time to wait for my check to clear. And Pete Sanders' bosses weren't thrilled at the idea of taking a three-by-six-inch piece of paper from a stranger and letting him drive away with one of their cars. Pete finally came up with the idea of driving me to an ATM where I could make a withdrawal on my checking account. The receipt would, and did, show that I had sufficient funds to cover my check.

With a car to get there, Joyce and I now had to identify somewhere in Baton Rouge to stay. All our researches came up empty. Every hotel room in the city and for hundreds of miles around was occupied. New Orleans was closed, so the hotel residents had no place to go, so we had no reason to hope that hotel space would become available anytime soon. Finally, on

Saturday, September 3, Joyce called a sorority sister, Mary Lou Potter, who lived in Baton Rouge with her husband Bill. Joyce and Mary Lou had remained close for some time after college, but they had gradually lost touch, and it had now been some years since they'd been in contact. From almost any perspective save the desperation caused by Katrina, calling Mary Lou seemed a preposterous act of imposition: Hi. How are you? May my husband and I come and live in your home for an indefinite period?

At that time, officials were speculating that the city might not be habitable for six months. Hi. How are you? Would you mind if we moved in with you for half a year? Of course, because Bill and Mary Lou are among the finest, most selfless people I have ever met, they encouraged us to come on. We arrived on September 5, and the Potters opened their home to us. They gave us keys. They fed us. And through absolutely no fault of Bill and Mary Lou, Joyce and I have never felt so vulnerable, so helpless, so lost.

While Joyce and I were driving to Baton Rouge, Tim Ryan and Joel Chatelain were making a daring journey to the UNO campus to procure the financial records we needed to pay people and the Internet information we needed to rebuild communications. Standing, as it does, just south of Lake Pontchartrain's levees, UNO is on relatively high ground. Our campus took flood water only on the southernmost part of our property along Leon C. Simon Boulevard. At the height of the flood, UNO was an island. And because it was dry and empty, the Coast Guard had, after rescuing them from rooftops, deposited 2,400 people there, directing them, so we were told, to break into our buildings for shelter and raid our dining facilities for food. They left these increasingly desperate people there without additional communication for four days before finally transporting them to staffed and supplied shelters elsewhere in the country.

These refugees were all gone by the time Tim and Joel decided they had to get to campus. But widespread (and frequently hysterical) reports of violence had thoroughly spooked the Coast Guard as they escorted Tim and Joel, by boat from Bucktown in Jefferson Parish, to the dock near our lakeside Research Park. Both UNO administrators were outfitted with battle helmets and flak jackets and were protected by a phalanx of riflemen as they made their way on campus to get the computer records we needed. The military muscle was unnecessary. The campus was empty. But the mission was a smashing success. Tim and Joel weren't able to bring back everything we could have used, but they brought back crucial electronic information that made our recovery quicker and less complicated than it otherwise would have been.

While the other institutions of higher education in New Orleans quickly suspended operations for the fall term of 2005, almost immediately upon gathering in Baton Rouge, our administrative group decided that we would try to restart a fall semester in early October. UNO owns a three-story former office building on Causeway Boulevard in Metairie, and though it had sustained considerable wind damage to the roof and attendant water damage to interior walls from rainfall, it had not flooded. So we decided to offer as many classes as possible at what we call the Jefferson Center, to schedule additional classes at night in public school buildings in dry areas of the region, on the north shore of Lake Pontchartrain and the west bank of the Mississippi, and to put as many courses on line as student demand might warrant.

Eventually, we settled on a restart date of October 10, and our entire team of chancellor, vice chancellors and deans and other senior administrators devoted the five weeks after reuniting in Baton Rouge to achieving our reopening. Though our sister school, LSU Baton Rouge, is housed in more than 250 buildings spread across a 2,200-acre campus, the LSU System provided us with two rooms from which to rebuild our university. The space we took to calling the Boiler Room housed a bank of phones and two dozen computers. Faculty and staff who could find accommodations in Baton Rouge worked in the Boiler Room communicating our plans to faculty who had evacuated elsewhere and ultimately assisting our far-flung students with advising and registration.

The second room we called the War Room, formerly the conference room for the system's human resources division. The room was designed as meeting space for perhaps 12, but became the day-long working space for 22 crowded around the oval table in the room's center or facing the wall on tiny desks jammed into the room's four corners. Here, the chancellor, the provost, the vice-chancellors, the deans and other senior staff had as much "office space" as was taken up by a laptop and a square of table top for a cup of coffee. From these spaces we ran the university for a month and a half. We were advised by system officials to begin laying off employees immediately, but we were determined to pay as many of our faculty and staff as were willing to work for as long as we had money to do so.

Led by the efforts of our Director of Federal Affairs, Rachel Kincaid, we were determined to acquire enough emergency Congressional funding to balance the 2005-2006 budget into which Katrina had ripped a gaping hole. State officials warned us sternly that these efforts would not succeed, but ultimately they did, and we were able to avoid forced layoffs during fiscal 2005-2006. On October 10, 2005, we reopened at the Jefferson Center, at our high-school sites and on line. Joel Chatelain and Metropolitan College Deans Bobby Dupont and Carl Drichta deserve especial acknowledgment for getting the Jefferson Center sufficiently repaired in time, and, as it was, our faculty had to teach for several weeks in dusty classrooms where sheetrock did not reach all the way to the floor. But while all the other universities in New Orleans remained dark during the fall of 2005, UNO taught 7,000 students, and 766 graduated when the fall term ended. They graduated and thereby were able to take the next steps in their lives, into the work place or on to graduate school. Of all the many moments that I will cherish about my UNO career, none is more important than our graduation ceremonies at the end of the fall 2005 semester. And those days of standing together and defying the odds will remain, for all of us in the War Room and the Boiler Room, among the finest days of our lives.

———————————

About a week after Joyce and I moved into Mary Lou and Bill's guest room, I was notified by LSU System Vice President Caroline Hargrave that she had secured a room for me and Joyce at the LSU Faculty Club. There were many ways in which remaining with the Potters was a superior living option. Their home was beautiful and spacious and located on a gorgeous lake. At the Potters' we had access to a kitchen and laundry facilities for our shorts, jeans and additional clothing we'd purchased at WalMart. We had comfortable furniture in which to lounge or read. And unlike the Faculty Club where we'd have to pay for our room, the Potters never mentioned, and I am sure would have been aghast at the very concept of, asking us to pay rent. But the Faculty Club was just minutes from my new work space at the LSU System office, whereas the commute from the Potters' house was taking over an hour. Moreover, despite our hosts' boundless generosity, Joyce and I were simply too old to be comfortable in someone else's house, particularly someone's house where we had invited ourselves to live. So we gratefully took Dr. Hargrave up on her connection at the Faculty Club and moved there where, for the first time in two weeks (counting the days at my mother's), we could finally have our own private space.

The feeling of comparable freedom lasted until we were told by Faculty Club management that we would have to move out by noon on September 22. "It's the Tennessee game," I was told by way of explanation. All over the state, people now living in hotels were sometimes running into problems with long-term residence, so much so that Governor Kathleen Blanco had quickly issued an executive order restricting management from evicting their residents. In a hem-haw way, I pointed this out to the manager of the Faculty Club. "I'll be glad to make a reservation for you again next week," she responded. "You just have to move out for the weekend. I'm sure you understand: it is the Tennessee game."

And there you have one of the more enduring things I gradually and with abiding resentment came to understand about the dominant culture at LSU Baton Rouge. Tiger football trumps all else. I may have been the number two executive officer at the second largest university in the state, a sister institution to LSU. I may have been at the moment homeless. My energies may have been needed in trying to resurrect my school. But if I had ever dared to entertain such an idea, I was entirely wrong that the office I held and, more important, the institution I represented, resided in the same universe of concern as Tiger football. People who had their own homes to live in and their own beds to sleep in had football tickets and thus had made reservations at the Faculty Club long before my house had the discourtesy to surrender itself to Hurricane Katrina and my school the impudence to lose all its students in a finger snap. Surely I understood: it was the Tennessee game.

———

Using guile and exercising chutzpah, Joyce and I were able to make a crucial trip to New Orleans on September 13, 2005, two weeks after the flood waters rose into 80% of the homes in our city. We had been studying the situation in our neighborhood as best we could through satellite images that had been posted on the Internet. These photographs were amazingly clear and frustratingly indistinct. We could see the roof of our house. And we could see water surrounding the structure. We found a website that estimated the depth of the water in our neighborhood at over five feet. But was that in the center of the street? By the curb, which was lower? Or did that figure represent the amount of water on our property? Almost every inch of difference in meaning might prove critical.

Built in 1926, our house is a Mediterranean "high-low" or split level. The living room, dining room, powder room, den and kitchen are built with floors exactly four feet six inches above the ground, which, in turn, is about six inches above the level of the street. These rooms stand over a dirt crawl space. Behind the living-room level, stand a two-car garage and three ground-floor rooms rising to a height of exactly seven feet. The house's bedrooms and full bathrooms are built above the ground-floor rooms and garage, connected to the living room floor by a flight of six stairs. The ground level houses a utility space for a washer, dryer, water heater and freezer as well as a bathroom and a bedroom that Joyce had converted to her home office. Accessed by concrete steps from this area is an eight-foot deep mechanical pit, set into the ground just like a Midwest basement. The mechanical pit contains the house's air-conditioning and heating systems and is protected by a ledge around the top that is one-foot high and one-foot thick.

We had lived in our house for 12 years when Katrina struck, and, despite several torrential rainstorms that had paralyzed the city with flooding during that time, we'd never had a drop of water in the garage or ground-floor area, much less in the ledged mechanical pit. If, however, Katrina's breached levees had let much over a foot and a half of Lake Pontchartrain brine into our neighborhood, then the pit ledge would be topped and our heating and cooling systems would be destroyed. From the satellite photos we had seen, and from the web estimates we had studied, we assumed that the pit was flooded and would remain so even after emergency pumps had drained the water from the yards and streets of our neighborhood. Thus, when we set off from Baton Rouge on September 13, we did so only after our friends Elia Diaz-Yaeger and Michael Yaeger volunteered to assist us by arranging to borrow a gasoline-powered pump and a pickup truck to haul it in. We went down in two vehicles, the Yaegers in the truck, Joyce and I in the used Ford Explorer we'd bought in North Carolina.

New Orleans was still officially closed on September 13, and would remain so for days longer. But the National Guardsmen that had been mobilized to patrol the streets and minimize burglary and vandalism were letting workmen and journalists through their blockades. Michael and Elia in the white Ford pickup with the pump were workmen. With a business card from *Gambit*, the weekly paper for which I have written a column of film criticism since 1980, I was a journalist. Joyce was my assistant, my photographer, I would claim, if need be. We were stopped on Interstate 10 about 20 miles outside the city but were waved through the roadblock without much inspection. At the city boundary, Michael and Elia were waved through a checkpoint without comment. A guardsman stopped us and made me show my "credentials." He took my card and held it close to his nose. "What's *Gambit*?" he asked. "A newspaper," I replied. "You a writer?" he said, handing the card back to me. "Yeah," I said, and he shrugged, waving me through.

The New Orleans we found 17 days after leaving it was a messy place. We had to dodge downed trees almost every block, but clearly some agency had dragged enough debris aside to make some streets passable. Two things struck us immediately when we got out of our vehicles at our house on Versailles. Our summer lawn and those of our neighbors should have been a deep, dense green, but instead they were all brown. And the air smelled like mildewing hay. The city was eerily quiet, and almost totally empty. We worked eight sweaty hours at our house that day, but the only person we saw the whole time was a helmeted, rifle-toting National Guardsman on patrol in his battle fatigues, checking homes for dead bodies.

Hope is an amazingly resilient quality of the human psyche. All evidence suggested we were in for bad news when we opened the door to our house, and, with our pump, we had come prepared to deal with what we could of it. Nonetheless, Joyce and I confessed to each other later, that we'd each dared to hope the water inside had not topped the one-foot ledge that protected the mechanical pit. This was, in essence, to hope that what we knew to be true was, somehow, not true. Each of us knew that such a hope was crazy, and that's why we didn't share it with each other beforehand. But each of us clung to that hope all the same.

What we found inside our house was worse than we'd dared hope but better than we deeply feared. The watermark on the ground floor stood at 39 inches, and indeed the mechanical pit was full to the brim with sludgy black brine. The heating and cooling systems were lost, as were the washer, dryer, water heater and freezer on the ground floor. Joyce's office was beyond recovery. The old desk she had in the room had collapsed, dumping her papers and legal files into the muck. We found them in gluey clumps on the ruined hardwood floor. The worst news was in the garage. Utterly beyond repair, our cars had become colorful and perhaps toxic terraria. Sickly orange mushrooms sprouted from the ulpholstery and steering wheels, while powdery golden mold grew on all surfaces save the glass.

But upstairs the news was better. The water had stopped short of reaching the living room floor, though the hardwood floors were slick with green mildew, which also crept up the wooden legs of our furniture. Using the disinfectants that we'd brought with us from Baton Rouge, Joyce and Elia wiped away mildew, while Michael and I fired up the pump and drained the utility pit with a hose we snaked out of the house and around to the street. Getting the pit drained as soon as we did almost certainly saved us from a major, costly and demoralizing mold infestation in the upstairs areas of our home. As it was, all the clothes in our closets smelled dank and looked green until they were washed or dry cleaned.

Every weekend for the rest of September, Joyce and I bluffed our way into the city and worked on our house, first throwing things away in fetid heaps identical to those that pockmarked the city everywhere for the next year, then tearing out tongue-and-groove walls and taking the ground floor down to bare stud, then spraying mold killer on every surface that remained, then spraying a second time and a third. All of this labor was exhausting and numbing. Much of it was dispiriting as we saw formerly valued possessions, furniture, clothing, golf clubs, household tools, Christmas decorations, all ruined by flood waters, piled in the street until scraped away by earth movers and dumped into refuse trucks.

But, as we should, Joyce and I count ourselves among the lucky. We remember with gratitude the generosity of our friends Ray and Sharon Mize who let us stay on weekends at their house in Kenner, which had escaped the flood waters, and who labored long, dirty days at our sides, emptying out the flood's ruin and dealing with the appalling foulness of full refrigerators left closed and without power for a month before we could deal with them. And we place our losses in the perspective of those who lost much more. Our house would ultimately need an entirely new roof, and, like everyone whose residence flooded, we had to have our electrical wiring replaced. We had to purchase and install new HVAC systems and ductwork and new appliances throughout the house. But our insurance was good and relatively quick. Our uninsured losses we would once have considered staggering, but now understand as manageable.

Meanwhile, across the city, hundreds of thousands of our fellow citizens lost much more. In our own immediate professional circle, Chancellor Ryan, our Vice Chancellor for Research, Bob Cashner, Vice Chancellor for Advancement, Sharon Gruber, Dean of the Library, Sharon Mader, Associate Provost Dennis McSeveney and too many of our faculty and students to list specifically, lost their homes entirely along with all their possessions, including photographs and other keepsakes that documented the courses of their lives.

When UNO defiantly succeeded in reopening its doors at the Jefferson Center on October 10, 2005, Joyce and I gave up our room at the Faculty Club and took up residence at her family home in Carrollton's Riverbend section, which had not flooded. From that beachhead we hired the workers we needed to make our many required repairs, and we moved back into our house on Christmas Eve, four months after fleeing, lucky beyond a doubt since so many of our fellow citizens have not been and will never be able to return to their homes and, in many cases, the lives they led before the storm.

———

On October 17, 2007, after buying a sandwich for lunch at a reopened restaurant on Elysian Fields near the UNO campus on October 17, 2007, I decided to take a short drive through the surrounding Gentilly neighborhood. What I found, more than two years after the storm, was not encouraging, more than two years after the storm. In a five-block stretch between Prentiss Avenue and Robert E. Lee Boulevard, I counted in this once vital area, nine vacant lots where houses used to stand and 24 homes that appeared to have been abandoned. Rebuilding was underway in only eight homes, and only three houses appeared to be occupied. In the vicinity, both St. Raphael Catholic School and Avery Alexander Public School were closed and boarded up. No rebuilding was underway. In a nearby commercial area along Elysian Fields, the grocery, the Chinese restaurant, the convenience store, the dry cleaners, the bakery and a health clinic were either shuttered or demolished.

This appalling lack of progress is the direct result of ineptitude and worse on the part of our local, state and national governments. And this small segment of Gentilly near the UNO campus is not exceptional. In neighborhood after neighborhood throughout the city, homes are windowless, abandoned, forlorn—properties melting into uselessness like soft plastic figurines left atop a hot stove. So short a time ago, each of these decaying edifices was someone's home where good, spicy food simmered in the kitchen and the laughter of full lives echoed within its walls. Now the air smells of mold and mildew, and inside the walls silence reigns. Ruined lawns, broken sidewalks, rubble-strewn vacant lots and streets breed despair, house to house, block to block.

The sorrow we face is registered in every destroyed school, its playing children vanished, in every church where hymns are no longer sung, in every store where goods are no longer sold, in every café, restaurant and bistro where our good food is no longer served and where friends no longer gather. There is no excuse that this devastation has not been repaired because it could have been. Clear-headed, responsible, decisive, caring leadership at all levels of government could have brought New Orleans much closer to recovery than it stands today.

Consider a series of situations on the UNO campus. When we returned to full-time operations on our main Lakefront campus in January of 2006, housing for our students was a major concern. Our Privateer Place Apartments were still being repaired, and our Lafitte Village for married students was completely out of commission. Privately-owned apartments in the area were everywhere uninhabitable as was true throughout much of the city. So UNO arranged with a FEMA contractor to place 400 trailers on our property, in the green space along Elysian Fields and in the parking lots on the western edge of campus. These trailers could have accommodated three students each. But a snarl of bureaucratic red tape began to knot almost immediately after the trailers were delivered. Throughout the spring term of 2006 they sat together empty as a taunt to students who were either paying exorbitant rents to live in the city or commuting to school from many miles away. The trailers were never hooked up to electrical, water or sewerage lines, thus never occupied, and in the summer of 2006, the FEMA contractors brought in their fleet of Ford F-150 trucks and hauled them away.

Also in the spring of 2006, because we registered only 12,000 students, UNO was forced into financial exigency, a state of dire fiscal emergency faced by very few institutions in the entire history of American higher education. The State of Louisiana was, in fact, running a huge budget surplus. But because UNO had lost students due to the storm, the university's state appropriation was cut by $6.5 million dollars. Added to the lost tuition revenues, UNO faced an annual operating deficit after June 30,

2006 in excess of $20 million. Just three miles away, the Southern Baptist Convention decided to shield its New Orleans seminary from required staff reductions due to lost tuitions for several years. Louisiana could have done the same for UNO and barely nicked its surplus. Instead, UNO was forced to eliminate 83 faculty lines and make other staff layoffs. Although not all the individual layoff decisions were mine to make, execution of the exigency plan fell extensively on my shoulders, and I will carry the burden of the decisions I was forced to make during that time for the rest of my days.

Now, 26 months after the storm winds died away, Katrina still stands stubbornly in our midst. Our University Center remains only semi-functional, its lovely atrium blocked with scaffolds, its ballrooms, meeting rooms and offices out of commission. Reconstruction could have rendered it fully restored in less than six months, but state bureaucracy has kept the project even from going to bid, despite FEMA's commitment to pay. Work on our west-side dining facility, the Cove, has also yet to begin. Our married student housing remains shuttered. Our arena will only be completed in the late spring of 2008, out of operation for three academic years. Federal money has been earmarked for all these projects, yet state red tape prohibits our recovery from moving forward beyond a snail's pace. This is appalling, and it is inexcusable. Why should UNO students be condemned to have their educational experiences diminished in this way? And one thundering question stands out: Is there a single soul in the State of Louisiana who believes that identical facilities at the so-called flagship LSU campus would remain unrepaired and out of service in November of 2007 if Hurricane Katrina had struck Baton Rouge rather than New Orleans in August of 2005? A single soul?

A single soul?

A comparable inquiry must be made about our city as a whole. Recent reports out of our nation's capital reveal that Louisiana, and therefore New Orleans, was shortchanged in the allocation of federal recovery funding. A disproportionate amount of the recovery money was dedicated to Mississippi where a Republican governor maintained close relations with the Republican White House. Katrina was a disaster which should have called upon our elected leaders to rise above the usual infighting of their political affiliations. But that didn't happen, and the residents of this city are suffering from it to this day, still waiting for the lesser amount of money that has been set aside for them to actually be paid to them so that they can begin rebuilding their lives.

In sum, we New Orleanians know something about the great flood of 2005 that America as a whole has never fully grasped. It was a disaster made not by nature but by man. The waters of Hurricane Katrina did not sweep over our city; they broke through to our city. Our levees were high enough, but they were not strong enough. Our homes were lost, our lives were altered, not as an act of God, but as an act of negligence, not as the product of inevitability but as the byproduct of irresponsibility. Moreover, it was a disaster that didn't end when the flood waters were pumped back from whence they came or a few weeks or months later. It is a disaster that isn't over yet, and from the perspective of fall, 2007, it is a disaster that may not be over for years to come.

Yet, in whatever atmosphere of sadness and indignation, we fight on, as the voices in this text testify. And about my fellow citizens of this unique city, I think of language from Shakespeare's *Henry V*, for Katrina was our St. Crispin's Day and we will forever fiercely "stand a tip-toe when the day is named… and strip our sleeves to show our wounds… we band of brothers" and sisters who suffered together, who have received inadequate assistance, but nonetheless refuse to surrender.

———

Immediately upon arriving at LSU System headquarters on September 6, 2005, I began to tell the story of my evacuation and listen to the stories that my friends and associates had to tell of their experiences. That process of story exchange still takes place today. History will readily record the length of the breaches, the level of the water, the number of evacuees and the percentage of the city that was damaged. But only in the individual stories will the extent of this disaster be understood. Everybody who lived in this city has a story, and everybody's individual story is a critical part of Hurricane Katrina's whole horrible saga.

Already on September 6, 2005, I began to want to capture as many of those stories as possible and to preserve them in our UNO library for scholars to study in the future. In the days that followed I asked the students in our creative writing program to write their own narratives and to be agents for gathering the narratives of others. My thanks to Joanna Leake and Gabrielle Gautreaux for their early leadership in this project. In the semesters that followed, many UNO faculty used their classes to generate narratives as oral history, writing, sociology, anthropology and other projects. With fear that I may overlook important contributions well worth acknowledging, my thanks to Professors Pam Jenkins, Vern Baxter, Rachel Luft, Valerie Gunter and Connie Atkinson. Thanks also to Bill Lavender who has embraced new duties as director of the UNO Press and to his hardworking staff including Barbara Johnson, Erin Gendron and David Parker. Thanks also to editorial assistants Jennifer Violi and Zachary George. But the book that contains these reflections belongs to Rebeca Antoine who selected, arranged and edited the narratives. Without Rebeca's drive, commitment and editorial acumen, this volume simply would not exist. And, of course, my ultimate thanks to all whose stories are told herein and to the survivors who have lent their voices to our shared history.

November 12, 2007

Interviewers and Writers

Editor **Rebeca Antoine** was born in Connecticut and is a graduate of Yale University and the Creative Writing Workshop at the University of New Orleans. Her fiction has appeared in numerous venues, most recently in *The Briar Cliff Review* and *GulfStream*.

Missy Bowen was born in Minnesota. She manages operations for the University of New Orleans Department of Music and hosts a blues show on WWOZ-FM.

Susanna Dienes is a native New Yorker. She received her B.A. from The New School for Social Research and her MFA in Creative Nonfiction from the University of New Orleans. Currently, she and her husband reside near Washington, D.C., where they fell in love during the Katrina evacuation.

Amy Ferarra-Smith was born and raised in New Orleans. She is an editorial associate in the Diocese of Pensacola-Tallahassee Office of Communications and a writer for Florida Catholic. She lives in Navarre, Florida, with her husband, Justin.

Zachary George is an MFA student at the University of New Orleans, currently living in Prague, Czech Republic.

Eileen Guillory lived with her elderly grandmother in the Gentilly Woods neighborhood until the storm destroyed their home. She received her undergraduate degree from Loyola University in New Orleans and is a graduate student at the University of New Orleans as well as a history teacher at the Louise S. McGehee School.

Jana Mackin was born in Sebastopol, California. A published poet, journalist and avid Cubs fan, she received her B.A. from the University of California at Santa Barbara, her M.A. from San Francisco State University, and her MFA at the University of New Orleans. She lives in New Orleans and Butte, Montana.

Carol McCarthy was born and raised in Chicago. She currently lives in New Orleans with her husband and puppy and is working toward her MFA in poetry at the University of New Orleans.

Matthew Peters graduated from the University of New Orleans in 2006 with an MFA in Creative Writing. Participating in the Katrina Narrative Project helped him overcome the grief of losing his Gentilly home. Although he and his wife have relocated to Orlando, they still miss New Orleans. He is currently working on a book to help others overcome catastrophic loss.

Amy Judith Reuben Pickholtz is originally from Toronto, Canada. She lived in New Orleans for 15 years before Hurricane Katrina relocated her to Prairieville, Louisiana where she lives with her husband and their new baby and pusues her MFA degree from the University of New Orleans.

Nicole Pugh is a writer, editor, teacher and performer who lived in New Orleans until Katrina. She now lives out of a suitcase between San Diego, California and Hawaii.

Sylvia Schneller, MD, retired from a 35-year practice of psychoanalysis and is now pursuing her MFA in Creative Writing at the University of New Orleans. She is the recipient of the 2007 first place prize for nonfiction and the third place prize for fiction from The Gulf Coast Association of Creative Writing Teachers.

Caroline Skinner returned to New Orleans, her native city, after working for several years in New York. Now residing in Bellefonte, PA, a small victorian town in the Allegheny mountains, she is writing her MFA thesis while waiting tables.

Mary Sparacello is pursuing her MFA in Creative Writing at the University of New Orleans, focusing on creative nonfiction. She is a native of Omaha,

Nebraska, and graduated from Brown University in 1998 with degrees in English and History.

Kristin Schwartz was a graduate student in sociology at the time of the storm. She has since graduated and lives outside New Orleans on the north shore of Lake Ponchartrain.

Dena Vassey taught at Frederick A. Douglass High School in the Ninth Ward of New Orleans for two years. She met her husband in the Crescent City, and they returned there to wed in 2006. They now live in Augusta, Georgia with their daughter, Myda.

Sheila Willis takes boxing lessons three mornings a week to deal with Katrina stress. She received a paralegal certificate from the University of New Orleans in 2000 and continues to pursue her B.A. degree while working full time. She lives now in Covington, Louisiana with her husband and dreams of attending Loyola Law School in New Orleans.